Alfred Frederic Falloux, H. W. Preston, Anne-Sophie Swetchine

The Writings of Madame Swetchine

Alfred Frederic Falloux, H. W. Preston, Anne-Sophie Swetchine

The Writings of Madame Swetchine

ISBN/EAN: 9783337172503

Printed in Europe, USA, Canada, Australia, Japan

Cover: Foto ©ninafisch / pixelio.de

More available books at **www.hansebooks.com**

THE WRITINGS

OF

MADAME SWETCHINE.

EDITED BY

COUNT DE FALLOUX,
OF THE FRENCH ACADEMY.

TRANSLATED BY H. W. PRESTON.

BOSTON:
ROBERTS BROTHERS.
1869.

Entered according to Act of Congress, in the year 1869, by
ROBERTS BROTHERS,
In the Clerk's Office of the District Court of the District of Massachusetts.

CAMBRIDGE:
PRESS OF JOHN WILSON AND SON.

TRANSLATOR'S NOTE.

THE favor with which the "Life and Letters of Madame Swetchine" was received by the public, has induced the belief that some portion of her graver writings might also awaken general interest. No woman of our time has felt more deeply, or reasoned more keenly, on subjects of supreme moment, than she; few women of any time have possessed in a more remarkable degree the gift of gracious and vivid expression. The story of her early doubts and struggles was told in the previous volume: in this we have the fruit of her self-conquest, the gentle admonitions of her ripened wisdom, the last serene results of her rich opportunities and her reverent life. It is hoped that these pages may find a welcome with all who love experimental no less than speculative truth, and who recognize the essential unity, under whatever name or form, of all profound religious experience.

HARRIET W. PRESTON.

DANVERS, Sept. 1, 1869.

TABLE OF CONTENTS.

	PAGE
PREFACE	1

AIRELLES.

KLUKVA PODSNEJNAIA	3
AIRELLES	4
ON MUSIC	34
ON THE FIRMAMENT	35
ON NATURE	36
ON COURTESY	38

THOUGHTS.

CHAPTER I.

ON HERSELF. — ON GOD. — ON THE SOUL. — ON THE INTELLECT 41

CHAPTER II.

ON THE WORLD. — ON THE AFFECTIONS. — ON DIFFERENT AGES. — ON POLITICS 57

PAGES SELECTED FROM AN ALBUM	82
ON THE REPROACH OF EXCLUSIVENESS AS INCURRED BY THE CATHOLIC CHURCH	84
ON THE CHURCH AND HER FORM	87

ON OLD AGE.

COMPILER'S DEDICATION	92
NUNC DIMITTIS	130
CHRISTIANITY, PROGRESS, AND CIVILIZATION	131

ON RESIGNATION.

	PAGE
PREFACE	142

CHAPTER I.
On Resignation apart from Christianity . . . 144

CHAPTER II.
The Justice and Propriety of Resignation. — Its Different Degrees 162

CHAPTER III.
On the Advantages of Submission 174

CHAPTER IV.
On Resignation to so-called Irreparable Ills . 186

CHAPTER V.
On the Difficulty of Resignation to Sorrows caused by our Fellow-beings 198

CHAPTER VI.
How, in the World and out of it, Every Thing and Every Being, except Man, accomplishes God's Will, and keeps in the Place assigned it 211

CHAPTER VII.
That there is an Excess of Grief which belies the Words of Submission 223

CHAPTER VIII.
Is Resignation compatible with Prayer, that God will remove the Evil which afflicts or threatens us? 241

CONCLUSION 251

WRITINGS OF MADAME SWETCHINE.

COMPILER'S PREFACE.

THIS volume contains what may be called the works of Madame Swetchine, unless that term implies a degree of premeditation which she never entertained.

The pages denominated "Airelles,"— a title of Madame Swetchine's own selection,— and those only, were carefully collected by herself, and copied into a small volume.

The "Pensées," and the succeeding pages, even those which bear the name of "Treatise," were written at different times, without any fixed plan or reliable dates, upon loose leaves, thrust successively into an envelope, or rolled into a shapeless bundle, and confined by a pin. The writing is invariably very rapid, and often almost illegible, much of it being in pencil.

The "Treatise on Old Age" was far from being finished according to the author's ideas. It was necessary, before publication, to cut out certain fragments, which were but summary indications of points of view to which Madame Swetchine proposed to return; also some unfinished inquiries and imperfect sentences.

The "Treatise on Resignation" is more connected and complete. It is divided into chapters, which have already received their titles: but it is not finished; and the multitude of indices shows us that the author intended to retouch it in every part.

This labor, now of correction, now of co-ordination, — always deeply respectful of Madame Swetchine's own primary thought, whenever it is distinctly revealed, — has required prodigious sagacity, patience, and devotion. I have a right to insist upon these merits, for they are in no sense mine. Constant trouble with my eyes has prevented me from reading or writing for several years; and I have been obliged to call to my assistance other friends of Madame Swetchine, who have been willing to be mine as well.

I should not allow myself this personal confidence, did not the strict fulfilment of my duty towards these friends require it. I had only one way of discharging my debt, — to place their names beside hers.

I venture to hope that the public will sympathize with my feeling, if I select each one of my fellow-laborers for a tribute of gratitude with regard to that portion of the work which he has especially helped to illustrate.

A. DE FALLOUX.

AIRELLES.

KLUKVA PODSNEJNAIA.

(AN AIRELLE[1] WHICH HAS BEEN UNDER THE SNOW.)

THIS Airelle is distinguished from all the others by its shape and its corolla. It is common in all the northern marshes of Europe, Asia, and even America, where it creeps over the moss with its loosely trailing stems. It blossoms in Russia in the month of June, and the fruit ripens in October; but it is tart at this season, and to sweeten it, they let it remain under the snow through the winter, and gather it the ensuing spring. Hence its name, *podsnejnaia*, — that which has been under the snow.

Under the auspices of this simple flower, I have placed the following thoughts. They, too, have ripened under the snows, and taken their hue, like this little red berry, from the fires of the interior sun. The most of them were committed to writing during the winter of 1811, which I passed in the country, in profound retirement. They are utterances which sprang from my own heart, but reached no other; impressions which clothed themselves in images to people my solitude.

---

[1] The Vaccinium Vitis Idæa, or Cowberry.

AIRELLES.

I.

Let our lives be pure as snow-fields, where our footsteps leave a mark, but not a stain.

II.

In the season when nature is despoiled, there is no lightest breeze or breath of wind which is not strong enough to detach the leaf from the tree which bore it. So, in the autumn of the heart, every movement deprives us of a joy or a hope.

III.

To reveal imprudently the spot where we are most sensitive and vulnerable, is to invite a blow. The demi-god Achilles admitted no one to his confidence.

IV.

Happiness and Vice are mutually exclusive : Happiness and Repentance mutually prejudicial. Happiness and Virtue clasp hands and walk together.

V.

When fresh sorrows have caused us to take some steps in the right way, we may not complain. We have invested in a life annuity, but the income remains.

VI.

The mind wears the colors of the soul, as a valet those of his master.

VII.

There are souls which, like the pontiffs of the ancient law, live only on the sacrifices they offer.

VIII.

There are people who never speak of themselves, for fear of interrupting their own introspection.

IX.

With how many futile signs and superstitious inductions do we not associate our destiny, when impelled by a strong need of happiness! All nature then seems to conspire for or against us; and there is no one of her secrets which does not appear to be mysteriously connected with our own. Poor humanity! so dependent, so insignificant, and yet so great! Who has not seen, on those green plains, where the peaceful flocks graze with all the ease and dignity of tranquil possession, the intelligent being, — the being who is superior to all the magnificence of creation, — subordinating all his hopes for the future to the destiny of a few leaves left motionless, or carried away by the wind; following with unquiet eye the course of a cloud, or calling on the daisy to declare the sentiments of his beloved.

X.

The second Paulus Æmilius had two sons: the first died three days before his father's triumph; the second, three days after. Such is the universal fate of man. He dies before he is happy, or has but a few days in which to be so.

XI.

The beings who appear cold, but are only timid, adore where they dare to love.

XII.

It would seem that by our sorrows only we are called to a knowledge of the Infinite. Are we happy? The limits of life constrain us on all sides.

XIII.

In retirement, the passage of time seems accelerated. Nothing warns us of its flight. It is a wave which never murmurs, because there is no obstacle to its flow.

XIV.

What is resignation? It is putting God between one's self and one's grief.

XV.

There is an English song beginning, "Love

knocks at the door." He knocks less often than he finds it open.

XVI.

Those who have made the strength born of passion conducive to their return to virtue, are like the people in the neighborhood of Vesuvius, whose dwellings are constructed out of the very lava which threatened to destroy them.

XVII.

Exaggerated expressions do not chord with the idea, and wound the ear of an exact mind.

XVIII.

Those who have suffered much are like those who know many languages: they have learned to understand and be understood by all.

XIX.

We may say of many Christians, whose actions do not correspond with their words, "The voice is Jacob's voice, but the hands are the hands of Esau."

XX.

There are but two future verbs which man may appropriate confidently and without pride: "I shall suffer," and "I shall die."

XXI.

"Do not pity him: he is to blame." Harsh and revolting expression! He is to blame. The words excite my keenest and most tender compassion. The innocent, when oppressed by fate or by man, has two unfailing asylums, God and his own conscience. But the guilty dares neither lift his eyes to the God whom he has offended, nor descend into himself, where he encounters a manifold remorse. His last and sole refuge is our pity. Ah! let us esteem and admire persecuted and ever triumphant virtue; but let our tears fall upon the sores of conscience like the Samaritan's oil.

XXII.

How difficult is purity to the pure! A little pollen is enough to rob the lily of its whiteness.

XXIII.

If it were ever allowable to forget what is due to superiority of rank, it would be when the privileged themselves remember it.

XXIV.

That mysterious stone on which Jacob reposed was faith. Let us, too, sleep on its breast, and our future greatness will be revealed to us.

XXV.

We do not judge men by what they are in themselves, but by what they are relatively to us.

XXVI.

Impassioned characters never attain their mark till they have overshot it.

XXVII.

Conscience is, at once, the sweetest and most troublesome of guests. It is the voice which demanded Abel of his brother, or that celestial harmony which vibrated in the ears of the martyrs, and soothed their sufferings.

XXVIII.

The literature of Russia is a little like that iron money of Lacedæmon, which had no circulation out of the country.

XXIX.

There are questions so indiscreet, that they deserve neither truth nor falsehood in reply.

XXX.

The symptoms of compassion and benevolence, in some people, are like those minute guns which warn you that you are in deadly peril.

XXXI.

O widow's mite! Why hast thou not, in human balances, the immense weight which celestial pity accords thee?

XXXII.

One may make a solitude in the depths of his own heart, in the midst of a dissipated and worldly life. He may also, when his isolation becomes oppressive, people that solitude with beings after his own heart, and adapted solely to his purposes.

XXXIII.

The magic gifts of Oriental romance, which benevolent fairies dispensed freely and at will, are, it may be, a fantastic image of those more real boons which Providence has impartially distributed among all men. Thus, our volition recalls that mysterious ring which was endowed with creative power, — prudence, the talisman which anticipates or avoids danger; the imagination, the wonderful carpet which rendered all places present, and annihilated distance; resignation, finally, the universal balm, since it soothes and calms even the evils which it cannot cure.

XXXIV.

Humility is a cuirass which turns aside the blows dealt by the enmity of man; but that cuirass is defective at the heart.

XXXV.

There are words which are worth as much as the best actions, for they contain the germ of them all.

XXXVI.

Courtesy, in the mistress of a house, consists in feeding conversation, — never in usurping it. She is the guardian of this species of sacred fire, but it must be accessible to all.

XXXVII.

Misfortune is, like the honest man, as good as her word.

XXXVIII.

The qualities destined to subserve the happiness of others, remain too often idle and self-centred, like charming letters, which have never been sent.

XXXIX.

The injustice of men subserves the justice of God, and often his mercy.

XL.

Before Socrates, it was said, "Let us do good to those who love us, and evil to those who hate." Socrates changed the precept, and said, "Let us do good to our friends, and let us do no evil to our enemies." Only Jesus Christ says, "Bless them that curse you." It belongs to the Saviour of men alone, to train them to supernatural virtues.

XLI.

It is necessary, sometimes, to refrain from questioning our friends, that we may not draw from them what we ought not to know, and especially that we may not tempt them to deceive us.

XLII.

All the joys of earth will not assuage our thirst for happiness, while a single grief suffices to shroud life in a sombre veil, and smite it with nothingness at all points.

XLIII.

Let us desire no more intellect than is requisite for perfect goodness, and that is no small degree; for goodness consists in a knowledge of all the needs of others, and all the means of supplying them which exist within ourselves.

XLIV.

Mental culture and a well-regulated education assist the memory. An isolated idea is with difficulty impressed upon the mind; but when the newly acquired notion finds a point of contact already prepared in the intellect, it fastens upon what is analogous to itself, and forms, along with its antecedents and consequents, a chain whose very prolongation is the assurance of its strength. Here, as elsewhere, the richer one is, the easier it is to increase in riches; and here, too, the parable of the talents applies, "To him that hath shall be given, and from him that hath not shall be taken away even that which he seemeth to have."

XLV.

The smile upon the old man's lip, like the last rays of the setting sun, pierces the heart with a sweet and sad emotion. There is still a ray, there is still a smile; but they may be the last.

XLVI.

There are minds constructed like the eyes of certain insects, which discern, with admirable distinctness, the most delicate lineaments and finest veins of the leaf which bears them, but are totally unable to take in the *ensemble* of the plant or shrub. When error has effected an entrance into such minds, it remains there impregnable, because no general view assists them in throwing off the chance impression of the moment.

XLVII.

In the conflicts into which we are betrayed by passion, it is especially just to say, "*Væ victis !*"

XLVIII.

The most culpable of the excesses of Liberty is the harm she does herself.

XLIX.

Let us resist the opinion of the world fearlessly, provided only that our self-respect grows in proportion to our indifference.

L.

Alas for him, who, in the tranquillity of his heart, desires death, while there are yet sacrifices for him to make, happiness to secure, wants to anticipate, or tears to wipe away.

LI.

I would say of princes as the Protestants say of a higher Master, " service without worship."

LII.

If we devoted to the understanding of a thing the time we consume in appearing to have understood it, and listened all the while that we are revolving our own replies, would it not be better for the world?

LIII.

Our vanity is the constant enemy of our dignity.

LV.

Providence has willed that all the virtues should originate in actual wants, and all the vices in factitious ones.

LIV.

Love sometimes elevates, creates new qualities, suspends the working of evil inclinations; but only for a day. Love, then, is an Oriental despot, whose glance lifts a slave from the dust, and then consigns him to it again.

LVI.

We are always looking into the future, but we see only the past.

LVII.

It is by doing right that we arrive at just principles of action.

LVIII.

Indifferent souls never part. Impassioned souls part, and return to one another, because they can do no better.

LIX.

He who has ceased to enjoy his friend's superiority has ceased to love him.

LX.

Would you push the sinner to extremes, discourage the weak, and cause the sore heart to fester? Assume the uncompromising severity of stern and haughty speech, — and rest assured that the bad passions which provoke your zeal will redouble their violence. Oh, you who have surrendered your hearts to God, forget for a moment, if possible, your hatred of vice, if you would snatch away its victims! Animated by this sacred and consoling hope, let the wholesome knife, with which your hand is armed, penetrate, without tearing, the wound! Lift up, after you have cast down! Have ready pity for every fault, a ray of hope for every trial. Let not the unfortunate, as he leaves your presence, cry, "All is lost," (terrible words! they are hell in themselves!) but let him bless you as a comforter, and feel that all may yet be regained.

LXI.

The courage with which we have met past dangers is often our best security in the present.

LXII.

The chrysalis is a type of the old man. He vegetates, and is torpid; but he will live; and, during this slumber and temporary impassibility, the wings are forming which shall bear him on to immortality.

LXIII.

Loving souls are like paupers. They live on what is given them.

LXIV.

There are things which we cannot help knowing, but which we must never acknowledge.

LXV.

The most dangerous of all flattery is the inferiority of those about us.

LXVI.

The labor which perfects our intellectual faculties, while it develops, elevates, rectifies, and clarifies or dilutes our ideas, is the source of a wealth which tends to become inherent, and which positively augments our individual worth. Those acquirements which simply furnish the mind; which are imported into it without taking root, or adding any thing to its power and compass, are our property, indeed; but they are not ourselves; and they leave us, in point of moral value, exactly where they found us. Gold, tortoise-shell, and ivory may embellish a lyre; but these vain ornaments can never cause it to send forth full and sonorous tones.

LXVII.

To have ideas is to gather flowers. To think is to weave them into garlands.

LXVIII.

We estimate the virtue of others by its fruits; our own, by the sacrifices it enables us to accomplish.

LXIX.

Real sorrow is almost as difficult to discover as real poverty. An instinctive delicacy hides the rags of the one, and the wounds of the other.

LXX.

He who has never denied himself, for the sake of giving, has but glanced at the joys of charity. We *owe* our superfluity; and, to be happy in the performance of our duty, we must exceed it.

LXXI.

How can that gift leave a trace, which has left no void?

LXXII.

There are sinners whose justification is nowhere, and their excuse everywhere.

LXXIII.

In strong and thoughtful characters, the motives of action and conduct generally must be sought in fixed principles; while the ground of the ideas by which impetuous characters suppose themselves to be governed is found in the sway of passing impressions.

LXXIV.

" Is not life useful when it is happy ?" asks the egotist. " Is it not sufficiently happy when it is useful?" asks the good man.

LXXV.

Since there must be chimeras, why is not perfection the chimera of all men?

LXXVI.

" Prayer," says St. Jerome, " is a groan." Ah! our groans are prayers, as well. The very cry of distress is an involuntary appeal to that invisible Power whose aid the soul invokes.

LXXVII.

The chains which cramp us most are those which weigh on us least.

LXXVIII.

Virtue is the daughter of Religion: Repentance, her adopted child — a poor orphan who, without the asylum which she offers, would not know where to hide her sole treasure, — her tears!

LXXIX.

There are people who betray their friends a little, just for the sake of showing that they are faithful.

LXXX.

When Charity commands us to love indifferent persons "as ourselves," it doubtless authorizes us to love our friends better.

LXXXI.

Indulgence is lovely in the sinless; toleration adorable in the pious and believing heart. Modesty is especially becoming to superiority, affability to greatness, moderation and simplicity to wealth, and self-forgetfulness to those who never forget others. But the guilty, obscure, or commonplace man has too much interest in the goodness of others, for his own to be taken kindly. He is always in the position of an unfortunate debtor who is seeking to soften his creditor's heart; and, when any disposition is useful, it is rarely unsuspected. The virtuous man alone can be compassionate and generous at his ease.

LXXXII.

If we would go on to perfection, we must take care not to refer back to external causes our faults and deviations from duty, — even those which may be called accidental. Our faults are indeed our misfortunes; but their memory is a precious heritage; for they alone, it may be, cause us seriously to reflect. Let us not repudiate their moral teaching for the sake of ridding ourselves of their troublesome weight, but rather strive unceasingly to ascend from the effect to the cause within. Let us deny the involuntary theory, reject that of accident, and accuse none but ourselves. Let us take note of the misgivings of conscience, of impulses whose origin is obscure or suspicious, of nameless remorse. Let us note these things, and give ourselves no uneasiness; — "The Lord knoweth them that are his."

LXXXIII.

Let us ever exceed our appointed duties, and keep within our lawful pleasures.

LXXXIV.

The freest and the most despotic governments represent the two *régimes* under which religion is most needful to man. In the first, there is an excess of life, and of development of the individual will, which may become a source of disorder and of danger if its exercise be not regulated by the restraints of an interior law. Under the second, which includes every variety of social evil, man cannot have too many of the hopes of heaven, or the consolations of earth, to enable him patiently to endure humiliation and misfortune.

LXXXV.

By becoming more unhappy, we sometimes learn how to be less so.

LXXXVI.

"Woman is in some sort divine," said the ancient

German. "Woman," says the follower of Mahomet, "is an amiable creature, who only needs a cage." "Woman," says the European, "is a being nearly our equal in intelligence, and perhaps our superior in fidelity." Everywhere something detracted from our dignity! It is very like the history of the dog! — a god in one country; muzzled or imprisoned in many others; and sometimes "the best friend of his master."

LXXXVII.

Those who make us happy are always thankful to us for being so. Their gratitude is the reward of their own benefits.

LXXXVIII.

It is not true that a strong feeling is necessarily exclusive. On the contrary, — a lively affection, if happy, brings into play our faculties of loving, and increases their activity outside the circle of the primary interest. Ah, how rich is the overflow of a softened heart!

LXXXIX.

We are early struck by bold conceptions and brilliant thoughts: later, we learn to appreciate natural grace and the charm of simplicity. In early youth, we are hardly sensible of any but very lively emotions. All that is not dazzling appears dull; all that is not affecting, cold. Conspicuous beauties overshadow those which must be sought; and the mind, in its haste to enjoy, demands facile pleasures. Ripe age inspires us with other thoughts. We retrace our steps; taste critically what, before, we devoured; study, and make discoveries: and the ray of light, decomposed under our hands, yields a thousand shades for one color.

XC.

"*Firenze non si muove, se tutta non si duole,*"[1] says an old Tuscan proverb. There are many souls like Florence.

XCI.

Our faults afflict us more than our good deeds console. Pain is ever uppermost, in the conscience as in the heart.

XCII.

Friendship is like those ancient altars, where the unhappy, and even the guilty, found a sure asylum.

XCIII.

I would sooner believe in a happiness born of tears, than in a joy which should be compatible with aridity of soul. The obstacles to the bliss of a loving heart are external. The hard heart bears them within; and the more immediate cause has also more certain effects. A few plants still lift their moist heads above

---

[1] If Florence is moved, all things suffer.

inundated plains; but the sands of the shore are always sterile.

XCIV.

We expect every thing, and are prepared for nothing.

XCV.

A good, finished scandal, fully armed and equipped, such as circulates in the world, is rarely the production of a single individual, or even of a single coterie. It sees the light in one; is rocked and nurtured in another; is petted, developed, and attains its growth in a third; and receives its finishing touches only after passing through a multitude of hands. It is a child that can count a host of fathers,—all ready to disown it.

XCVI.

Suspicion has its dupes, as well as credulity.

XCVII.

In the first part of life, we give every thing to others, and expect every thing from them.

XCVIII.

Repentance is accepted remorse.

XCIX.

The doctrine of compensation is one of those whose truth becomes ever more and more apparent; but those who are blessed with outward advantages, are not to appropriate it without hesitation, or maintain it without caution. It would ill become him who has been happy in the long run (though every day may have brought its trials) to insist upon an equilibrium which seems to have been disturbed in his favor. It is on the lips of the poor and oppressed that this truth becomes powerful, and serves the cause of virtue by reminding us of the noble and saintly joys which God has ordained by way of counterpoise to grief, misery, and despair.

C.

A good action leaves behind it an impression of seemingly incompatible effects. On the one hand, it attaches us to life; on the other, it strengthens us against death. In the first instance, it mediates between us and our sorrows; in the second, between God and our sins. The Christian is the only man who can, logically, both love life and desire death; and have we not here the secret of that sovereign good which Plato sought?

CI.

Parodies, on things I love, either disgust me, or trouble my conscience. Nothing that has touched the heart ought ever to be profaned.

CII.

Men do not go out to meet misfortune as we do. They learn it; and we, — we divine it.

CIII.

It is marvellous to think how much cannot be done by those who can do every thing.

CIV.

Devotion, like genius, has its feats of daring.

CV.

All chains weary: and if we shake them, they gall us. God doubtless has permitted this, that one yoke may be easy, and one burden light.

CVI.

Let us not fail to scatter along our pathway the seeds of kindness and sympathy. Some of them will doubtless perish; but if one only lives, it will perfume our steps and rejoice our eyes.

CVII.

When Friendship asks for her share, Love is always disposed to answer, "You will have nothing while I live." — "Ah, well, my Lord; I can wait!"

CVIII.

There is nothing at all in life, except what we put there.

CIX.

Strength alone knows conflict; Weakness is below even defeat, and is born vanquished.

CX.

In each new trial, we must seek for the chastisement, or the warning, which it implies. Every external event is a fable which illustrates some moral truth.

CXI.

"Moi seule, — c'est assez."[1]
The "moi" of Medea, is "God" for the Christian.

---

[1] I alone am sufficient. This a quotation from Corneille's Medée, and the entire passsage is as follows: —

NERINE.

Forcez l'aveuglément dont vous êtes séduite,
Pour voir en quel état le sort vous a réduite:
Votre pays vous hait, votre époux est sans foi.
Dans un si grand revers que vous reste-t-il? —

MEDÉE.

Moi!
Moi, dis-je, et c'est assez —

NERINE.

Quoi, vous seule, Madame?

MEDÉE.

Oui, tu vois en moi seule et le fer et la flamme,
Et la terre et la mer, et l'enfer et les cieux,
Et le sceptre des rois, et le foudre des dieux.

Of this passage, Voltaire says, —

"Ce *moi* est célèbre. C'est le *Medea superest* de Sénèque. Ce qui suit est encore une traduction de Sénèque." — TR.

CXII.

Man's inclination is to know all; to understand all, even at the price of his own happiness. Has he been wounded by a few isolated words? He regrets that he was unable to seize their connection. Has some trifling anxiety ruffled the surface of his heart? He cannot rest till he has reduced it to a melancholy certainty. In short, — were misfortune at hand under her most fearful aspect, wrapped in the folds of a triple cloak, his consuming instinct would force him to remove them all.

CXIII.

It is a mercy to the rich that there are poor. Alms is but the material life of the latter: it is, at least in a degree, the spiritual life of the former. If the rich could not give, they might still be charitable: the heart has a thousand ways for that; but the portion of wealth which they retain, would no longer be purified, ennobled, and sanctified by that which they dispense.

CXIV.

Love enters the heart unawares: takes precedence of all the emotions, — or, at least, will be second to none, — and even reflection becomes its accomplice. While it lives, it renders blind; and when it has struck its roots deep only itself can shake them. It reminds one of hospitality as practised among the ancients. The stranger was received upon the threshold of the half-open door, and introduced into the sanctuary reserved for the Penates. Not until every attention had been lavished upon him did the host ask his name; and the question was sometimes deferred till the very moment of departure.

CXV.

Only a just appreciation of things will enable us to possess them tranquilly, or console ourselves for their loss.

CXVI.

The world has no sympathy with any but positive griefs. It will pity you for what you lose; never for what you lack.

CXVII.

It is only in heaven that angels have as much ability as demons.

CXVIII.

There are not good things enough in life to indemnify us for the neglect of a single duty.

CXIX.

Intellectual pride is less outraged by the obscurities of faith than by the authority with which it is clothed.

CXX.

There are people who never give their hearts: they lend them, and always at high interest.

CXXI.

Moral difficulties — the perplexity attendant on conflicting interests and duties, between which we cannot choose, and dare not decide — have often made me think that it is the will of Providence to impose mysteries upon the conscience, as well as the mind. On the one hand, we have the faith that submits blindly; on the other, the heart humiliated, because it cannot take refuge in the certainty of having done right.

CXXII.

Kindness causes us to learn, and to forget, many things.

CXXIII.

Pride dries the tears of anger and vexation; humility, those of grief. The one is indignant that we should suffer; the other calms us by the reminder that we deserve nothing else.

CXXIV.

I would rather choose my griefs than my joys, because I dread the former more than I anticipate the latter.

CXXV.

A woman who has never been pretty has never been young.

CXXVI.

Let us guard against touching those strings whose ready and sad vibration carries us back to a time of lost happiness. The conquerors of Scotland endeavored to insure their peaceful possession of the country by interdicting to her bards those pensive, yet stirring, airs, wherein yet lingered all the power of the olden time.

CXXVII.

Silence is like nightfall. Objects are lost in it insensibly.

CXXVIII.

There is nothing steadfast in life but our memories. We are sure of keeping intact only that which we have lost.

CXXIX.

Attention is a silent and perpetual flattery.

CXXX.

I can understand the things that afflict mankind, but I often marvel at those which console. An atom may wound, but God alone can heal.

CXXXI.

Servility is almost always worse than insubordination.

CXXXII.

If it were allowable to use proper names, how easy it would be to make out a list of the ninety-and-nine just persons, whose safety causes less joy in heaven than the repentance of a single sinner!

CXXXIII.

Travel is the frivolous part of serious lives, and the serious part of frivolous ones.

CXXXIV.

There is a rapture, an eloquence, a brilliancy, and an animation of the mind, which belongs peculiarly to youth, and corresponds to that condition of the body which is called "La beauté du diable."

CXXXV.

It is possible to be cured of every thing and sick of nothing.

CXXXVI.

Power is the act; authority, the right. The one compels, — the other induces, submission.

CXXXVII.

We want justice from indifferent persons, and partiality from those we love. And the more such partiality transcends our deserts, the more evident is the source of so sweet a misconception.

CXXXVIII.

We are rich only through what we give, and poor only through what we refuse.

CXXXIX.

Nothing can be more insolent than some forms of indulgence. There are people who absolve you with the air of having the right to condemn.

CXL.

In youth, we feel the richer for every new illusion; in mature years, for every one we lose.

CXLI.

What a difference it makes in private relations, whether one is irreproachable, or merely unimpeachable!

CXLII.

No two persons ever read the same book, or saw the same picture.

CXLIII.

We are often prophets to others only because we are our own historians.

CXLIV.

There is a transcendent power in example. We reform others unconsciously when we walk uprightly.

CXLV.

Men are always invoking justice; and it is justice which should make them tremble.

ON MUSIC.

Harmony and melody — which have an equal share in the effects produced by sound — find their original type, it may be, in the double nature of the universe, and of human destiny considered socially and individually. Harmony, like the external world and its moving masses, presents us with various parts, linked together and arranged so as to subserve one and the same end. Regular and measured in its movement as the celestial orbs, — no deviation is allowable even in its boldest flight. An almighty will seems to have bound it to magnificence and grandeur, restricting its freedom to the latitude of the laws whose expression it is. But melody is thoroughly moral, and consequently free. It is the heart's utterance, and follows and renders its emotions faithfully. When brilliant, it recalls our joys; when sweet and lingering, it portrays our rare and delicious intervals of repose. It sighs for our disquietudes and sways beneath our sorrows, like a friend who shares them. Would it reproduce the sad and vague yearnings which by turns agitate and soothe the soul of man? — its songs are as dreamy as his chimeras. Melody is but one thought at a time, but — mobile and rapid — it renders all thoughts in succession and tells the tale of a complete destiny. Harmony, with its grand effects, seems made to appeal to assembled men; melody, to transport the memory in solitude. Words may of course be adapted to a piece of pure harmony; but they are only accessory, When melody is associated with human speech, they rival one another in charm and in power. Speech is, indeed, the heart's expression; but melody remains its accent.

ON THE FIRMAMENT.

Is it not amid the rigors of winter that the celestial vault impresses us most deeply as the region of the immutable and the eternal? Type of the world of souls!—there is no trace of time in that kingdom of space. There is beauty without spot or wrinkle, —immortal youth. Like the soul, the sky has dates, but not age. Like the soul, it has no night, but changes its lights as the soul varies in brightness. The succession of the seasons causes the vicissitudes of the earth,—its burning heats and hoary frosts, its long and sad intervals of desolation. But, by a sublime immunity, the heaven, although created, knows neither change nor decay. In the day-time, waves of light burst from its glowing central fire; in the night its dark depths sparkle with innumerable suns. The mighty immobility of its planets, or their triumphal march beneath the watchful gaze of the Most High, seem to image the impassibility of the saints or their swift and irresistible zeal. Thus, while nature—bound beneath the yoke of the winter solstice, desolate, mute, hiding her nakedness in a shroud — seems to accuse man of sin and its fatal consequences; the sky remains blue; the sun keeps the gold of his beams, the moon her silver clearness, the stars the blaze of their many-colored diamonds: in a word, the vault of heaven, resplendent and gloriously arrayed, seems like the heart of the good man to celebrate a perpetual feast, — the feast of the promised restoration. Kindly mother though she be, the Earth sometimes allows her breasts to dry; but the fount of light never fails, — the world could not live else. Again and again the day dawns and the shadows flee away, that we may be lured to the sweetness of a hope in the future. Nothing is irrevocable, within or without us. The cloud parts, the mist rises, the vapor disappears; and the trustful, hopeful, watchful observer is comforted. Power is watching over him, under the form of imperishable beauty.

ON NATURE.

The diverse aspects of nature, like the manifold meanings of art, are so many voices which penetrate the heart and speak to the intelligence. Every thing in the visible world, — the world which we see and hear, — expresses the heart's thought or responds thereto. 'Tis the old story in another language; for nature, too, is what the fall of man has made it. Its scenes and effects have a mysterious analogy with the dispositions we bear within, — both with those we would resist and those whose triumph we would secure. The result of the connection is, that this inanimate, insensible nature is not without its effect on us, — that our moral impressions depend upon it and it does us good or harm. According to the page which arrests our attention in this great book of nature, we find ourselves modified. By turns, it strengthens or seduces us, troubles or calms; causes to circulate in our veins the pure air of the mountains with its swift and buoyant life, or the perfumed breezes of the valley with their perfidious softness. We yield to the influence of the phenomena which it displays in our sight. Thus, its grand perturbations unsettle us: a terrible fatality seems to urge us toward the yawning chasm. The rocks, piled and jagged, like petrified tempests, remind us of other terrible and lasting ravages. Vertigo seizes us on steep and lofty heights; and a close and narrow horizon fatigues the eye, which requires space as the soul requires a future. The sublime majesty of the ocean or the Alps transports us, enchants us, gives us glimpses of other heavens beyond the clouds; yet soon the need of rest, even from admiration, forces itself upon us. In consequence of this reaction, when urged by a longing for strength and peace we fly the foaming, hurrying torrent, — the running stream which makes us dream too much, — the river which flows into the distance. Instinctively, and as if to assure the free possession of ourselves, we pause on the shore of those peaceful lakes, — those wonderful sheets whose aspect, at once solemn and serene, raises the tone of our meditations. In such a tranquil and harmonious mood, nothing appeals or responds to us more perfectly than those shadowy tarns hidden in the recesses of the mountains, whose glassy surface is another azure sky. What thought and feeling does it not awaken, — that solitary, remote, silent, nameless lake? Pure, limpid waters in a verdant cup, — a single glance takes in their charming unity. Living, but restrained within limits which they cannot pass, they seem like wisdom reconciled to necessity. Ask the lake the secret of its deep inner life, and it answers by the rich vegetation of its border. Life and its blessings are everywhere on its banks, and in its bosom; danger, nowhere. The wave upon its surface stirs not the golden sands of its bed; it hides no ruins, for it has seen no shipwreck.

ON COURTESY.

Courtesy in the world is by no means a false and culpable pretence. It softens rather than dissimulates; and, on the whole, since it deceives nobody, it cannot be accused of falsehood. Incompatibility of character; the profound and radical differences which are born of principles drawn from hostile sources; the eager pursuit of conflicting ends, — all these elements of discord, brought into play by the lively irritability of self-love, wounded pride, or opposing interests, make it hard to understand why the assembling together of men is not oftener the occasion of strife, invective, and bitter provocation. Yet the effect, in our *salons*, is very far from corresponding to the universal cause. Without greatly vaunting its motives, urbanity comes to our aid. By the blandness of its forms, it supplies the place of the justice and moderation which ought to reign within. The most decided opinions are shorn of all outward acerbity; and, while they do not entirely cease to manifest themselves, yet, by suppressing all show of hostility, and moderating their forms of expression, they are enabled to inflict no mutual wounds, but to pass one another, — like two clouds charged with electricity, — near enough for recognition, but not for contact. This species of *sordino*, imposed upon the sentiments, might easily have the effect of hardening in error a mind trained in an inferior civilization; and which, accustomed to a different diapason, might mistake for indifference, laxity, or scepticism, the forms which are made supple to avoid needless friction. For those who can read in this dim light, a word, an interval of silence, an illusion ever so remote, the slightest change of intonation, suffice: and the result is, that, if no one expresses his thought exactly as he feels it, no one stops at the precise form of expression; but the clear and actual sense is discovered, and remains in the intellect only, — as the nude may be distinguished beneath the drapery. If we study politeness in its models, we shall find that it never leads, — I will not say to falsehood, but to the slightest concession even; and that, to a practised eye, the genuine thought disengages itself in perfect integrity from the forms by which it is surrounded. Doubtless, a just toleration, a disposition to respect the ideas and convictions of every free and intelligent being, would be preferable to arrangements which are but skin-deep; but a spirit of deference at once steadfast, sincere, and enlightened, belongs to a perfection so rare that the majority of men must remain strangers thereto. A less lofty principle of action is needed; and such a principle is expressed in that system of delicate calculations and permissions which has received the name of *savoir-vivre*, — perhaps because it is the condition of all mixed, social life.

THOUGHTS.

COMPILER'S DEDICATION.

To M. L'Abbe de Cazales and Comte Jules de Berton, with the grateful acknowledgments of A. de Falloux.

CHAPTER I.

ON HERSELF. — ON GOD. — ON THE SOUL. — ON THE INTELLECT.

I.

I LOVE knowledge; I love intellect; I love faith; — simple faith yet more. I love God's shadow better than man's light.

II.

It is singular, — the tendency of many pious minds to grant an easy entrance to all that borders on the supernatural. My own disposition is the very reverse of this. It is faith which preserves me from credulity.

III.

I love God as if he were alone in the universe. I pity the human race as if there were no God. There is an abyss between these two extremes, which is bridged by our Lord and Saviour Jesus Christ.

IV.

In the matter of good-pleasure I love none but God's. That is always good.

V.

I tell thee of every thing, O my God! I engage thee in all my occupations. I invite thee to share in all my interests. It is so simple, can it be over-bold?

VI.

If one were to ask me the idea which I derive, from my own experience, of the happiness of heaven, I should answer, "Heaven is to love in peace."

VII.

I feel toward God as they say the Russian women feel toward their husbands; the more he beats me, the better I love him. That is all the devil gains by my chastisements.

VIII.

I have too often departed from God; but — praised be his name! — I have never separated myself from him.

IX.

Resignation is, to some extent, spoiled for me by the fact that it is so entirely conformable to the laws of common sense. I should like just a little more of the supernatural in the practice of my favorite virtue.

X.

My God, forgive me, and do what thou wilt!

XI.

My sole defence against the natural horror which death inspires, is to love beyond it.

XII.

"What!" said some one to me during one of my severe neuralgic attacks, "can you love a God who tries you so?"—"Ah, Madame! it is not a rare thing. I love one who makes me suffer."

XIII.

My God! cause me to do something which thou canst reward!

XIV.

O God, my destiny is in thy hands! I place it there! I would place it there if it were elsewhere! I will ever renew the act of placing it there!

XV.

God sees all. After years of accumulated suffering, can I wish to-day that I had never suffered?

XVI.

The solemn, wonderful, majestic ocean! It exalts, but only to crush me under a sense of its grandeur, — boundless, everlasting, pitiless of my insignificance. Wherein does it differ from me? In immensity of breadth and depth. What does it give me? A sense of infinity, and of the abyss which divides me from it. The ocean, in its might and unresting immutability, in the proportions which transcend the boldest flights of thought, is God, — but God without his Christ.

XVII.

The inventory of my faith for this lower world is soon made out. I believe in Him who made it.

XVIII.

I give myself up to God as one who knows that in justice God owes him nothing.

XIX.

I am my true self only in God's presence. My sorrows lie so deep, so far below the surface, that I have too little breath to bring them up.

XX.

I value time next to eternity.

XXI.

I have not another moment to lose or to waste. In the last days, we put the finishing touches. Thank God! I feel that I am in the right way. The banks seem to fly.

XXII.

Our relations with God are such that our obstacles are all means.

XXIII.

The fact that God has prohibited despair gives misfortune the right to hope all things, and leaves hope free to dare all things.

XXIV.

The events of life are a sacred text on which the mind may ponder and comment. How can we fail to follow with attention and respect — yea, often with gratitude and rapture — the chain of circumstances which has accomplished a thought of God.

XXV.

There can be no little things in this world, seeing that God mingles in all.

XXVI.

We recognize the action of God in great things:

we exclude it in small. We forget that the Lord of eternity is also the Lord of the hour.

XXVII.

Human life is an open book, where we read in every line a justification of God's law.

XXVIII.

What we comprehend of God is, not what he is in himself, but what he wills that we should comprehend. The treasure of divine knowledge is twofold: the full, entire, and final verity, which is God himself; and those minor verities — eternal, indeed, but only half revealed — which he enjoins, that is to say, imposes, on the children of men.

XXIX.

The Christian's God is a God of metamorphoses. You cast grief into his bosom: you draw thence, peace. You cast in despair: 'tis hope that rises to the surface. It is a sinner whose heart he moves. It is a saint who returns him thanks.

XXX.

My experience is, that Christianity dispels more mystery than it involves. With Christianity, it is twilight in the world; without it, night. Christianity does not finish the statue, — that is heaven's work; but it "rough-hews" all things, — truth, the mind, the soul.

XXXI.

To believe that aught can be needful which God denies, is a most stupid error.

XXXII.

Is the patient a physician, that he should choose his remedies?

XXXIII.

The obscurities of faith always permit us to see a little way into the impenetrable. They are a curtain which is never withdrawn, but which we are always lifting.

XXXIV.

Faith, amid the disorders of a sinful life, is like the lamp burning in an ancient tomb.

XXXV.

Piety is the guardian of faith.

XXXVI.

Piety softens all that courage bears.

XXXVII.

We must labor unceasingly to render our piety reasonable, and our reason pious.

XXXVIII.

The joys of religion are understood only by those who partake of them. Of all kinds of happiness, this is the one whose expression should be most moderate and humble in the presence of those who do not share it. "When you enter the house of a blind man," says an Andalusian proverb, "shut your eyes."

XXXIX.

Prayer has a right to the word *ineffable*. It is an hour of outpourings, which words cannot express, — of that interior speech which we do not articulate, even when we employ it.

XL.

Buffon has said, "The style is the man." The prayer also is the man, — the inner man. It is the *Ecce-Homo*, uttered, not to the Jews, but to God.

XLI.

We should abandon ourselves to God most entirely when he seems to be abandoning us.

XLII.

Our sins are as far transcended by the divine pity, as the innumerable by the infinite.

XLIII.

Salvation is a dual work. As in the incarnation,

there is implied a God and a man, — divine grace and human effort.

XLIV.

Christians are sometimes weak; but does any but a Christian ever strive to become strong?

XLV.

There is, by God's grace, an immeasurable distance between late and too late.

XLVI.

I allow the Catholic only one right; that, namely, of being a better man than others.

XLVII.

The saints, though rescued from the dangers which prove fatal to the majority of men, are still not exempt from conflict. The world has stolen from the interior life the law which ordains that a man can be tried only by his peers. Each one of us has a formidable personal foe; but it is much to have escaped the common Enemy.

XLVIII.

I like people to be saints; but I want them to be first, and superlatively, honest men.

XLIX.

The root of sanctity is sanity. A man must be

healthy before he can be holy. We bathe first, and then perfume.

L.

There are admirable examples which, when applied by the weak and faulty to their own case, are transformed into snares.

LI.

God has not chosen to flatter our curiosity by any of his revelations. What he reveals to man is the end assigned him, and the means of attaining that end. Doctrine and morals constitute an essential part of these means.

LII.

God has entrusted man with the raw material. He creates the world, and gives it to man to finish. Man originates nothing, but continues and develops all things. Speech is furnished him; and he invents writing. The ocean, fresh from God's hands, puts continents asunder: man makes it only the broadest of highways. The earth is delivered to him rough, and often sterile. He smooths and renders it productive. He grafts the wild stock. And, in the plan of salvation, the sufferings of believers finish and perfect the passion of our Lord.

LIII.

A miracle is medicinal, but never surgical; invisible in its action and known only in its results. You see it, you apprehend it; but you do not find that coarse evidence which precludes the slightest doubt. In religion, all is on the same plan. Light is ever mixed with darkness, — and why? That faith may be a virtue.

LIV.

If we look closely at this earth, where God seems so utterly forgotten, we shall find that it is he, after all, who commands the most fidelity and the most love.

LV.

How good it is of God, to have said in so many words in his gospel, "He that loveth father or mother more than me, is not worthy of me!" If these words had not been spoken for the eternal justification of those who rise above their natural affections, to what torture would it not have exposed hearts stung by the love of God! For their transports would have remained the same. Equally would they have been possessed by a feeling of the emptiness of all that is not God, and an impetuous and exclusive ardor for all that he is. The lever would have been as powerful as now; but, — with no support against flesh and blood in the express word of God, — how much doubt and uneasiness this ruling passion would have excited in their minds! They would still have loved as they love now; but they would have dissimulated in their actions, and concealed the living flame from all eyes, as men hide a shameful passion. God says decisively that he will be preferred. He does not merely permit: he enjoins it upon all, just so far as this sentiment may be reconciled with their other duties; and there are those for whom all duties are summed up in the gift of themselves to God.

LVI.

Pantheism, which confounds divine and human nature, has no more formidable enemy than the dogma of the incarnation, which unites them; for there is nothing more utterly exclusive of identity than union.

LVII.

The Church, — it is an inquiry for truth upon earth.

LVIII.

"Who will guard the guards?" says a Latin verse: "*Quis custodiet ipsos custodes?*" I answer, The enemy. It is the enemy who keeps the sentinel watchful.

LIX.

We can neither soar very high, nor dive very deep, without coming upon one of two regions fertile in truth; the realm of God's perfections, and that of man's misery.

LX.

In religious matters, moderation has its own criminals, — the neutral.

LXI.

Faith is best realized in sacrifice.

LXII.

The Catholic religion is like exuberant nature,— lavishing its treasures in the very desert, and in generous disproportion, not to the needs, but, alas! to the disposition, of those who profit by them.

LXIII.

Where the principle is right, God excludes nothing and sacrifices nothing; not the humblest virtue to the loftiest, not the smallest truth to the most sublime.

LXIV.

Miracles are God's *coups d'état*.

LXV.

The heart of the true Christian cannot be opened without there escaping thence gold, incense, and — alas! — myrrh also.

LXVI.

Nothing is exempt from the universal doom of degeneration and disintegration. Evil shows its head, its sharp tooth, its fang. A certain amount of evil is done; but it is limited and separable. The Redeemer is ever on the watch.

LXVII.

Defensive warfare, in the cause of religion, is the most noble of all; offensive, the most hateful.

LXVIII.

The Christian's cup may be brimful of sorrow; but for him the overflowing drop is never added.

LXIX.

When two conflicting truths are brought face to face, we must accept neither. We must tell ourselves that there is a third withheld among the secrets of God; which, when it is revealed, will reconcile them.

LXX.

The depths of the soul are a labyrinth, and dark without the torch of religion. Left to ourselves, we are like subterranean waters, — we reflect only the gloomy vault of human destiny.

LXXI.

There are souls, of every age and every clime, which are contemporaries and compatriots.

LXXII.

The very might of the human intellect reveals its limits.

LXXIII.

Our gains are proportioned to our possessions.

LXXIV.

Writing with a pencil is like speaking in a low voice.

LXXV.

It is but just that we should purchase our pleasures, but the moment when we pay is a hard one.

LXXVI.

Every better moment deepens our regrets.

LXXVII.

Language itself declares the inferiority of the collective to the singular. To begin with a Supreme example, compare what we feel when we say, the gods, and God; men, and man. And so in inferior matters: an assurance of *regard* is a promise of affection; to present one's *regards* is only an amenity. One may speak of his *friends*, without either having or giving the idea that he has a *friend*. *Respect* is a serious thing for him who feels it, and the height of honor for him who inspires the feeling; *my respects* are but a formula. An *interest* in life is all we can desire. Our *interests* are next to nothing. It is a pleasant thing to give occasion for a *compliment*. *My compliments* run at large. Everybody has *enemies*. To have *an enemy* is quite another thing. One must be somebody in order to have an enemy. One must be a force, before he can be resisted by another force.

LXXVIII.

Immortality! If man had it not, his soul would miss not merely the future, but the past; for these two are correlative. Without God and ourselves, the past would be nowhere. Nothingness would be behind and before us, and memory as vain as hope.

LXXIX.

Truth only is prolific. Error, sterile in itself, produces only by means of the portion of truth which it contains. It may have offspring, but the life which it gives — like that of the hybrid races — cannot be transmitted.

LXXX.

Let us never seek for truth outside the Church, nor leave it torpid in her bosom.

LXXXI.

The trace of original sin is found in every soul, like that of the deluge on the highest mountains.

LXXXII.

I see none but God who can reconcile us with the world.

CHAPTER II.

ON THE WORLD. — ON THE AFFECTIONS. — ON DIFFERENT AGES. — ON POLITICS.

I.

LET my terrace face the East! There is a mysterious affinity between this fancy of mine and my decided taste for the dawn of excellent things. Of all "rising suns" I except only that of prosperity; but I bow like a true courtier before the earliest rays of piety, virtue, and talent.

II.

When society is good for me, I need everybody; when bad, nobody.

III.

I love to please those who please me, and I do not hate to displease those who please me not. So I am sympathetic even in my antipathies.

IV.

Man always exaggerates his own importance, and underrates his own worth.

V.

The best advice on the art of being happy is about as easy to follow as advice to be well when one is sick.

VI.

Providence has hidden a charm in difficult undertakings, which is appreciated only by those who dare to grapple with them.

VII.

The gift of birth is a very different thing from the gift of life. To be born is to have every chance of a blessed immortality; to live is too often to forfeit them all.

VIII.

It is not true that heavy sorrows diminish our sensibility to trifling pains.

IX.

Misfortune has few riddles for him who believes that the sole design of Providence is the perfecting of mankind.

X.

A great sorrow does not always contain the ruin of a great joy.

XI.

In a healthy state of the organism, all wounds have a tendency to heal.

XII.

There is that in the impetuosity of passion, which precludes the idea of moral corruption. The waves of the torrent are troubled, and foam, and stir up the very mud of its bed; but only immobility makes water stagnant and induces that slow and general decomposition which alters the very essence of the element.

XIII.

I am not the one to be severe upon despair: I know too well how much courage is needed to resist it.

XIV.

The hidden good in the soul of a sinner would reconcile me to the guiltiest. The evil I encounter in the virtuous repels, and renders me inexorable. Do I excuse too much in the one case, and demand too much in the other?

XV.

Whenever there is any thing inexplicable in the conduct of estimable people, we must found our hypotheses on our esteem.

XVI.

Superior qualities are never conscious of themselves. Who ever thought himself humble without being made proud by that very fact? Does not generosity believe that it owes all it gives; and when did innocence ever know itself to be chaste?

XVII.

I can understand contempt for actions. Contempt for men I do not allow myself to feel; and I find no trace of it in holy writ. For who, let me ask, is the man whom we despise to-day? One whom we may be forced to admire to-morrow. In the infinite resources which God has placed in the depths of every human soul, there is a power of reaction, reparation, and rehabilitation, which transcends the utmost limits of evil. By God's grace the most abject of his creatures may rise to the rank of a celestial force. Only things that cannot change deserve contempt, — the void left by pleasures ardently pursued, the honors and emoluments which the sages of this world are so far from despising.

XVIII.

Consolation is not the business of our equals: the Master reserves that to himself. But we may learn the conditions which fit us to receive sovereign consolation.

XIX.

There is no place like a convent for keeping one's memories fresh, and the same is true of the country, though in a very inferior degree. In great cities, the absent are already dead; and the dead, as if they had never been.

XX.

If we would be equal to difficult undertakings, we must prepare for them long beforehand.

XXI.

There is a species of interlocutor who rides at anchor. His silence follows your speech, and he makes no attempt to comprehend or enter into it. You feel executed without being judged.

XXII.

The dilution of ideas which I love is intolerable to me. I like sugar, and hate sirup.

XXIII.

In the matter of criticism, I not merely respect severity in the examination of serious questions,— I like it: I do not want the cup sweetened. Only, truth upon one point necessitates the same upon all others, and blame expressed implies commendation wherever it is possible.

XXIV.

He who is not allowed to blame has a right to withhold his praise.

XXV.

Where there is a question of economy, I prefer privation.

XXVI.

When man revolts against the gospel, he takes another master, — himself: one who renders all inferior masters possible.

XXVII.

To do nothing is not always to lose one's time. To do what we do carelessly, is to lose it inevitably. It is weariness without profit.

XXVIII.

Situations are like skeins of thread or silk. To make the most of them, we need only to take them by the right end.

XXIX.

We have no right to force the conscience of him to whom we deny liberty.

XXX.

"Judge not," saith the Lord: the justice of which is obvious, in a world where there are no innocent to judge the guilty.

XXXI.

God himself allows certain faults; and often we may say, "I have deserved to err. I have deserved to be ignorant.

XXXII.

Let us shun every thing which might tend to efface the primitive lineaments of our individuality. Let us reflect that each one of us is a thought of God.

XXXIII.

We deceive ourselves when we fancy that only weakness needs support. Strength needs it far more. A straw or a feather sustains itself long in the air.

XXXIV.

We often need to ask advice; not always that we may follow it, but always that we may obtain more light.

XXXV.

Every one must find out for himself the key to the riddle of life. It is of no use to have it told. Some do not hear; others misunderstand it.

XXXVI.

What we need most is often the very thing we do not know. Often, also, we can make no use of what we do know.

XXXVII.

The best of lessons, for a good many people, would be to listen at a key-hole. 'Tis a pity for such that the practice is dishonorable.

XXXVIII.

We forgive too little—forget too much.

XXXIX.

We must do every thing for others; if only to divert our minds from what they fail to do for us.

XL.

Only those faults which we encounter in ourselves are insufferable to us in others.

XLI.

By entering into the thought of another, we reconcile him to our own.

XLII.

Our actual wants have definite conditions and limits. Our factitious ones obey no interior law, but run wild, without rule or measure. "Now that I am no longer hungry," said Mme. de Sevigné, "I will eat as much as you please."

XLIII.

Good is slow: it climbs. Evil is swift: it descends. Why should we marvel that it makes great progress in a short time?

XLIV.

One must be a believer, to combat superstition;

liberal, to contend against license; profoundly religious, before he can reprove fanaticism and extol tolerance.

XLV.

There are cases where a thing which is only reasonable, ceases to be so for that very reason.

XLVI.

Morality is the heart's truth; faith, that of the understanding.

XLVII.

Consolation heals without contact; somewhat like the blessed air which we need but to breathe.

XLVIII.

One who is very variable cannot be very sincere: to-day's truth is to-morrow's falsehood; or, at least, it is but a momentary sincerity.

XLIX.

We owe the truth to all who ask it; but, thank God, we are not obliged to convince them of it.

L.

Might we not say to the confused voices which sometimes arise from the depths of our being, "Mesdames, be so kind as to speak only four at a time"?

LI.

Situations where success is indispensable are bad. Those only are good in which the peaceful conscience can dispense with success, when all is done.

LII.

I once said to some one, "You represent to me that degree of moral worth which one must have, in order to deserve punishment."

LIII.

Philosophers say that causation plays a great part in the history of our faults, especially those of habit. It is in their causes that these must be attacked. We need to contend, not so much against the actions themselves, as the dispositions out of which they spring. Go back to the fountain, if you would purify the stream.

LIV.

It is not so hard as people suppose, to be faithful to one's engagements. The engagement which is to be kept, keeps you in its turn. It cuts hesitation to the quick, and protects the will with all the power of a promulgated decree.

LV.

Moral or intellectual evidence has other laws than physical evidence, but it is not one whit less authoritative. There is a species of proposition to which you must assent, as you must surrender when a hundred bayonets are pointed at your breast.

LVI.

If you speak the truth with moderation, — separating its substance from all alloy of human passion, — you are not to blame for the wrathful opposition it may encounter. But, if you strain it, if you wrest it from its sacred impassibility, if you do not maintain it with absolute sincerity, — you are responsible for the revolt which it excites, and for the consequences which may ensue.

LVII.

He who serves ideas rather than men is never deceived. Ideas may triumph, or not; but they never cease to be themselves.

LVIII.

That a man should enjoy publishing his writings, seems to me very natural. Ideas and facts belong to him. But greater reserve is, in my opinion, incumbent upon women, who have only their feelings to express, — for feeling loves a subdued light. When a man shows himself, he accomplishes his mission: to let themselves be seen is the utmost that is allowable, for the women of Europe.

LIX.

Why did the Invincible Armada perish, despite the beauty of its vessels, and the long-tried experience of its mariners? Probably the very fact that it called itself invincible had some share in its defeat. God allows us the epithet only after the fact.

LX.

Nothing can be replaced; for the excellent reason, that no two things are alike.

LXI.

We should never sin if we kept constantly before our eyes the Last Judgment, or even our own. The grand assizes of the valley of Jehoshaphat begin for us each day.

LXII.

We never do *very* well, except in those cases where if we did otherwise we should not do ill.

LXIII.

In this world of change, naught which comes stays, and naught which goes is lost.

LXIV.

Every time we have committed a fault, we must aim anew at perfection, — and all the more if the fault be a grievous one, — thus putting faith and trust in

God in the place marked by nature with discouragement.

LXV.

There is a certain water in the world whose taste never varies, be the hand that offers it constitutional, monarchical, republican, or autocratic. It is the holy water of courts. Everywhere you find it clear, colorless, and insipid.

LXVI.

When we see the shameful fortunes amassed in all quarters of the globe, are we not impelled to exclaim that Judas's thirty pieces of silver have fructified across the centuries?

LXVII.

The only true method of action in this world, is to be in it, but not of it.

LXVIII.

In the opinion of the world, marriage ends all; as it does in a comedy. The truth is precisely the reverse. It begins all. So they say of death, "It is the end of all things." Yes — just as much as marriage.

LXIX.

M. Ballanche says, that people must be of the same mind in order to dispute. It is very true; just as, to strike, one must be near enough for contact. The cannon-ball attains a vast distance; but, one hair's breadth beyond its range, its force is nil.

LXX.

It must be conceded that, after affection, habit has its peculiar value. It is a little stream, which flows softly, but freshens every thing along its course.

LXXI.

When two people agree upon fundamentals, even if they do not suit one another they have many points of contact. But this spiritual commerce is never like the sailing abreast of two ships on the open sea. It is a kind of coasting-trade from one port to another. No progress is made, and to meet is not to voyage together.

LXXII.

There are minds like those Chinese ladies who cripple themselves out of coquetry.

LXXIII.

The mysticism of the heart is of a better quality, and far safer, than the mysticism of the head.

LXXIV.

People who are in a hurry to speak have seldom any thing to say. Thought and ideas presuppose an intellectual effort.

LXXV.

Antiquity is a species of aristocracy with which it is not easy to be on visiting terms.

LXXVI.

The choicest of the public are not always the public choice.

LXXVII.

I have often seen pious persons very attractive to those who are not so. The life of piety, the unction it breathes, that interior prism radiating outward, exercise a charm inexplicable even to the hearts that feel it.

LXXVIII.

It was said of Mgr. Affre, — "He is hard and cold." Yes, — and so is marble; but beautiful things are made of it constantly.

LXXIX.

Whenever disparagement sums up by denying the existence of any given quality, you may be sure that the quality exists in some degree. "Such a one," people say, "has no mind." Yet he must have a little, or they would not take pains to establish the contrary.

LXXX.

Intolerance on the part of the philosophical and indifferent, — that most illogical combination, — reminds one of the jealousy of women who do not love their husbands.

LXXXI.

How many people are like dogs who seem to be looking for a master!

LXXXII.

It is under the seemingly identical influence of the same passion that the diversities of individual character come out. Pride leads one to what would be the extreme of humiliation for another.

LXXXIII.

Of how many people it may be said that their penetration is never quite subordinated to their sense of justice, save when it can promise them the pleasure of disapproval!

LXXXIV.

The great danger of gifted people is, that they are not much better assured than others against falling into error; while they have a great many more ways of rendering it harmful.

LXXXV.

When party-spirit, with all its passionate exaggerations, gets possession of a mediocre intellect, it deals the final blow. The poor soul never had light; and now it loses liberty. It must perforce return upon itself, describing ever narrower and narrower circles.

LXXXVI.

There are people whose good fortune it is, never to be deceived or undeceived save when their interest requires it. The way the right becomes dim or luminous to them is always marvellously opportune.

LXXXVII.

The great need of many is an interlocutor. They have listened, and then they have spoken, but they have never had an opportunity either to converse or to respond.

LXXXVIII.

Many friendships subsist on the reflection of one. To love deeply in one direction makes us more loving in all others.

LXXXIX.

The old friendships, — safe, genuine, and firmly built, — for which we take little thought, and which always avail us, are like those good thick walls of by-gone days; which need no repairs and are ever ready for shelter or defence.

XC.

There are hearts whose mere kindness sheds more rays than the love of others, as the moon of Naples shines with a softer splendor than many a sun.

XCI.

To love our friends is often not enough to satisfy them. We must also hate those whom they do not love.

XCII.

The ideal of friendship is to feel as one while remaining two.

XCIII.

Demonstrations of affection, in this world, are, for the most part, payment in counterfeit money. Yet some counters are better gilded than others.

XCIV.

A vast number of attachments subsist on the common hatred of a third person.

XCV.

What do we need to make us considerate? Much good sense, and a drop of pity in the heart.

XCVI.

We are amused through the intellect, but 'tis the heart that saves us from *ennui*.

XCVII.

The heart has always the pardoning-power.

XCVIII.

Youth should be a savings-bank.

XCIX.

A woman who consecrates her fidelity to a sinful affection is like those workmen who substitute Monday for Sunday.

C.

While we are still young, we enhance our youth coquettishly for this world's sake. When we are old, we think to deceive death so.

CI.

Years do not make sages: they only make old men.

CII.

In youth, grief comes with a rush and overflow, but it dries up, too, like the torrent. In the winter of life it remains a miserable pool, resisting all evaporation.

CIII.

A woman in years pleases an old man least of all.

CIV.

When we are old, we may sometimes enlighten, but we can no longer persuade.

CV.

Old age has nothing to expect from men, but every thing from God. Its helplessness is greater than that of infancy; for infancy finds universal sympathy with its weakness, but the only arm which can support the aged is the arm of the Lord. Despite his misery, the old man is like a king, — beholden to God alone.

CVI.

The void left by death is sometimes greater than the place filled in life.

CVII.

Unhappily, they only whose life is secluded, seek retirement.

CVIII.

The most conspicuous benefit of retirement is, that we issue from it ever more satisfied with God, and less satisfied with ourselves.

CIX.

Our habits, our external arrangements, our dwellings, and the order which we observe in them, are but the extension of our personality. We are all more or less like spiders, — stretching out a web made of our own substance.

CX.

We do not sufficiently consider that the genuine,

undisputed blessings — such as youth, strength, virtue, talent, and health — are blessings shared by all. With regard to these, there is no privileged class.

CXI.

So I must remain a fixture in Paris! What matters it, after all? The sky, the streams, the woods, — that is to say, God, his grace, and the safe asylum where we are flooded with its joy, — are not these everywhere?

CXII.

Railroads will greatly injure our dwellings; but, as to our affections, they can only harm themselves.

CXIII.

In the age in which we live, the impossible is every day losing ground.

CXIV.

Our age is so evidently an age of signal frankness, that even the apothecaries do not gild their pills.

CXV.

People read every thing nowadays, except books.

CXVI.

There are times when it would seem as if God fished with a line, and the devil with a net.

CXVII.

America has begun her career at the culminating point of life; as Adam did at the age of thirty.

CXVIII.

Revolutions use one to seeing in the vanquished of to-day the victor of to-morrow. The constant thought of surprises makes us instinctively provide for all times in one. There is no oblivion save that of eternity. We neither extol nor defend what is, and we smile at what may be.

CXIX.

France is so strong that she need proscribe but one thing, — proscription.

CXX.

However sound and loyal one may be, it is extremely hard always to side with the party in the midst of which one lives.

CXXI.

Those who undertake the government of a country with the avowed purpose of regenerating it, seem to me like women who marry in the hope of converting their future lords. The rashness of the enterprise would be more conspicuous, if the former did not, at all events, obtain power, and the latter a husband.

CXXII.

The real state of a nation or a man is as hard to determine as the true time. Every one goes habitually by his own watch, — M. Arago as well as another.

CXXIII.

God transforms, purifies, perfects. There are certain schools which can only mutilate, cut off, and destroy. God's mode of procedure seems to displease them. They like exclusion better than selection.

CXXIV.

I love the standard, but not the uniform.

CXXV.

Liberty must be a mighty thing; for by it God punishes and rewards nations.

CXXVI.

Liberty has no actual rights which are not grafted upon justice: and the chief duty of liberty is to defend justice.

CXXVII.

If the wind is not in the right quarter, nothing can be done. Danger itself has no threat or menace. It is the same in politics as in religion, when souls are to be converted. Till the hour of free grace strikes, the most persuasive voice, the best of books, the greatest orators, the tenderest whisper of the most ardent zeal, — all are powerless with the heart, which is not exactly hard, scarcely heedless, and by no means corrupt. It is somewhat like love, which comes when it pleases. In vain you accumulate torches. The damp wood smokes, perhaps, but it will not light; but, after a while, when the wind has dried it, a single match will set the whole in a blaze.

CXXVIII.

France has only repudiated incomplete and inconsequent doctrines. She awaits the signal which shall permit her to breathe in her institutions an air clearer than that of doubt, more strengthening than that of schism, holier than that of personal interest. The suitor for whom she waits is God.

CXXIX.

I see the earth tilled, but I do not see the seed.

CXXX.

France does not desire revolutions; but — whether she knows it or not — she desires revolution.

CXXXI.

Loyalty is patriotism simplified.

CXXXII.

I have never dreaded but one thing, — the absolute triumph of an individual.

CXXXIII.

I love victory, but I love not triumph.

CXXXIV.

It is difficult — and I would it were impossible — for a statesman to defend a line of policy contrary to his instincts and principles. There is a moral in a man's falling with the system he has sustained.

CXXXV.

When any one tells you that he belongs to no party, you may at any rate be sure that he does not belong to yours.

CXXXVI.

When men attain freedom for which they are unprepared, their faults are exaggerated. The strong become violent; the weak, lax.

CXXXVII.

There are two ways of attaining an important end, — force and perseverance. Force falls to the lot only of the privileged few, but austere and sustained perseverance can be practised by the most insignificant. Its silent power grows irresistible with time.

SOME PAGES FROM AN ALBUM

PRESENTED BY MADAME SWETCHINE

ON A MARRIAGE-EVE.

ALFRED has given you, dear Mary, a book containing your mutual vows, — a joint utterance which may well call down the blessings of Heaven upon your union. To this sacred volume permit me to add another, whose fair pages contain as yet only the image of her whose name you bear,[1] and who has been given you for a mother in heaven by your excellent mother on earth.

Thus, — while under the inspiration of the Church which has consecrated them, your hearts, clinging to the words of Alfred's book, shall soar heavenward with these, — I anticipate for my little album a destiny humbler, but not less sweet. Let it receive the confession of your spontaneous and inmost emotions, — of the pious thoughts which your very happiness shall suggest; for, if pleasure is rarely Christian, nothing is so justly dependent upon conscience as happiness.

---

[1] The Album opens with a picture of the Virgin.

My dear friends, I love to think that these leaves will "receive" your thoughts and feelings commingled, and that what is traced by the hand of each in turn will find a swift and sure echo in the heart of the other. What need of more than one word to express the thought of two hearts really united? From one and the same cup you are to drink the life that God has appointed you. *Sat una duabus.* The same page will yield you its reflections. Some day, long hence, these little records will assist you to go back the way you have come; and to retrace the duties you have accomplished, and the efforts you have made, together; — many a joy turned to profit; many a rapture concealed in sorrow, even, if sorrow has been freely shared; and all by means of living souvenirs and dates understood by you alone. And I, too, shall sometimes be associated with the little book which is to pass from my hands into yours. You must call to mind that, when I gave it you, I blessed you a thousand times; that, even before I knew you, dear Mary, I loved you, and that you had a share in my hopes before you crowned those of the heart that has chosen you.

Come quickly, then, and take your part, and double mine, in the sweets of a deeply cherished affection, and let me believe that some memory of me will always live in the fond and faithful hearts of you both.

MAY 12, 1841.

ON THE

REPROACH OF EXCLUSIVENESS

INCURRED BY THE CATHOLIC CHURCH.

———♦———

WHAT shall we say to the accusation of religious exclusiveness, which they bring against the Catholic Church? If it is to be understood in the sense of philosophical and logical intolerance, it may be remarked that the Church has this in common with every positive system; which by affirming truth on the one hand, necessarily implies error as its contradictory. The very existence of any given sect depends upon its preferring itself to all others; because the propositions to which, individually and collectively, it yields adherence, represent, for that sect, absolute truth. The sciences are no less positive in reference to the subjects of which they treat. How, then, is the Catholic Church *peculiarly* exclusive?

There is a religion, of which exclusiveness is the most striking characteristic, — the Jewish. It begins by concentrating all God's promises upon a single nation. It is exclusive; not because it believes itself in sole possession of the truth, but because it considers that the promises were designed for one particular race,—for men with the same blood in their veins, not for kindred spirits. Here, then, is actual exclusion; for it is plain that by no voluntary exercise, either of human or divine power, can a man be made to belong to a race, a tribe, a nation other than his own. Consequently, the religion of the Hebrews is less proselyting than any other. Confining all the promises to the children of Abraham, they cannot give foreigners a share therein. Moreover, the Jews live in the hope of the most incommunicable of all blessings; that, namely, of seeing the Redeemer born among them,—fruit of the womb of a daughter of David. Here all is fixed and unalterable, and has received the sanction of God himself. Prophecy is clear. Even if they wished to attract strangers to their faith, they could not impart the unrivalled glory promised them from the beginning of time. Here, truly, is exclusion, actual and authorized; actual through the very genius of the people, authorized by the promise that Christ should be born of the line of David.

But, if this epithet, exclusive, is eminently suited to the Hebrew faith, what applicability can it have to that religion which is, of all others, most opposed to its spirit? Opposed, not in the sense of hostility, but of contrast; opposed by the very spread of the truth, by the immense distance it has traversed, differing from it, in short, as the oak differs from the acorn.

Look at the very words, — an exclusive and universal religion; what an absurdity! Exclusive and proselyting! and so pre-eminently proselyting that the word, in its present sense, has been fully comprehended and applied by the Catholic Church alone! Exclusive! while she calls Greek and Scythian, Barbarian, Jew, and Mahometan; nor calls them only, but goes to them, opening her arms to all, ready to clasp and press them to her maternal breast.

ON THE CHURCH AND HER FORM.

"Jerusalem quæ ædificatur ut civitas; cujus participatio ejus in ipsidum. Illuc enim ascenderunt tribus, tribus Domini, testimonium Israël ad confitendum nomini Domini." — Ps. cxxii. 3, 4.

FORM, in its general and absolute sense, is never arbitrary. It is the strictest expression of the idea, its first and last *answer;* the characteristic of its substance; its utterance, also, in the sense of its manifestation. Determined in the realm of nature, by the quality and power of the internal principle, we behold the form ever faithful to the idea, as well in the intelligent as in the merely animate creation; both in the vegetable organism and in the mineral kingdom. Everywhere a primitive type; everywhere the creature rising in the scale of being in proportion as its form is more complete.

In painting and sculpture, whenever an artist would realize an idea, is he not bound to use every possible effort to preserve its peculiar character and give us a living manifestation of the thought? When marble and canvas glow under the might of an idea, what do they but materialize it? and is not the artist, though a free agent, *constrained* to bring it to our notice, to render it appreciable to our senses, to identify himself with it? Even in architecture, the most materialistic of the arts, is there not a necessary correspondence between the plan of the building and the use to be made of it; between the original design and the richness and variety of the material? Does not lyric poetry impress its own movement, accent, and rhythm on the music which accompanies it? and, in the drama, is not the music, which is the form, brought into almost servile subjection to the words? and are not the different human emotions always expressed in tones that are sad or sweet, solemn or joyous, as the case may be?

And, in purely speculative work, where thought confines its activity to its own peculiar sphere, is not the character of the expression regulated by that thought; and is not the merit of any creation determined primarily by the close and exact correspondence between the idea and its incarnation? The original choice, that of the idea, is entirely free; but, that choice once made, the elements which co-operate in its execution are, for the most part, given. The idea carries them, so to speak, within itself, and requires, in the expression, a true and faithful adherence to its nature.

If, then, it holds true in the arena of visible things, that persistent laws and unvarying conditions govern the realization and vivification of any thought or feeling, why may we not transfer these principles to the realm of religion, and conclude that there must be a fixed, unchangeable, absolute form, appertaining to a system of ideas unique, homogeneous, perfectly coherent, and without analogue upon earth? a system able to impose its authority upon the intellect, to conquer, to contend, to endure through ages; to endure,— nay, more,— to make war and to subdue. And if this order of ideas is God's revelation, can we suppose that the divine thought — while offering itself for the light, the guidance, and the support of humanity — would carelessly have abandoned to the caprice, the vain discussions, the fantastic choice, and the incessant unrest of that same humanity, the *form* whereby truth was to make herself known and impose upon the world her all-penetrating and all-embracing authority? By so doing, Providence would have accomplished but half his work; for, in lieu of dowering it with the conditions of durability, as he has done with his other works, he would thus have abandoned the loftiest and most necessary of them all to chance and the uncertainty of foreign aid. He would, indeed, have given man all, — and at what a price? — but so given that man must lose the fruit thereof. These same verities — if subjected to the fickleness and extravagance of the individual mind, without the defence of a sacred form, precise laws, and that aureole which marks and crowns the centre of power — could not have failed to become obscured, separated, and lost.

In an institution destined to last till the ages are consummated, all should be arranged with a view to unlimited self-support and self-defence. Even those who see in Christianity only a human invention, acknowledge that the strength of the church system, its internal administration, and the skill with which all the channels have been prepared through which its life circulates, explain, in part, its power of resistance. Those, on the other hand, who look at this wonderful institution from God's side, merely put divine wisdom in the place of human ingenuity, and see that, here as elsewhere, Providence has provided that the means should be adapted to the end.

In this choice and arrangement of constituent elements, what was involved? All Christianity. What would have become of its dogmas, without indefectibility to recognize them, unity to combine, and authority to insure them reverence? Only the Cœnaculum could be the continuation of Calvary.

I cannot forget, in this connection, an avowal wrung from one of the most powerful intellects I ever met, — a man who, born a Protestant, had become a Pantheist, and was wasting in the service of that system all the treasures of a rich and fertile imagination. This man, as commonly happens, rejected or distorted every aspect of Christianity; but he hated only Catholicism, one of whose glories it has ever been to receive the homage of hatred in default of that of love. In the midst of a long discussion, during which all the prejudices of his old error had cropped out from beneath the more recent stratum of his Pantheism, I arrested him with the question, whether he honestly believed that if the Catholic form had not existed in the world there would have remained of Christianity, after eighteen centuries of conflict, any thing more than a system of morals, — like Stoicism. After a few moments of silence, during which the face of my interlocutor assumed an expression which I see even now, he answered, "No: Christianity could *not* have lasted as a religion. It would have kept its place simply as a system of philosophic morality." Durability is the surest sign of strength, — its characteristic and its gage; and both strength and durability have their full development only in unity. Unity and perpetuity are nearly synonymous. "If man were one," said Hippocrates, "he would not die." The Church is one; and she will survive the earth. And what a magnificent thing is unity in plurality, — collective unity, — unity which does not preclude universality! Neither on the sword, nor on coercive force, does that union depend which is, in the language of a celebrated author, "exalted even to unity." All is free in the kingdom of mind, and obedience and love are one.

ON OLD AGE.

COMPILER'S DEDICATION.

To Count Paul Resseguier, with the Grateful Acknowledgments of A. de Falloux.

I.

OUR thoughts turn frequently to old age. Different moralists have made it the object of more or less protracted and elaborate reflection, but scarcely one has failed to touch upon it, and several have consecrated entire treatises to the subject. Induced, less by my growing years than by the feeling of gratitude that grows with them, to meditate upon old age, I find myself but seldom treading in the footsteps of others; and my wish is, to study this period of life in its connection with God and the life to come; to show that age is full of grandeur and consolation; that its activity is all the more intense for being brought to a focus; that no other situation can compare in dignity and beauty with this, in which the life of the soul is all; and that, in short, if the old man — as they say of the priest — is the unhappiest of men, he is the happiest of Christians, best prepared for the future, and, if he will, best comforted in the present.

Cicero amused his old age by making it a study; and this labor rendered the season smooth and pleasant to him. We are more fortunate than Cicero. With the eyes of Jesus Christ upon us, we feel that the sun has not wholly withdrawn his brightening, cheering, warming rays from the evening of our life.

Every age has its characteristic quality. Docility is that of childhood, whose whole moral code, like that of the world in its infancy, is comprehended in the precept of obedience. Youth is distinguished by self-devotion, maturity by strength, old age by dignity. Here are the full statistics of human life. Thou hast not, O my God, disinherited any age. Thou art lord of the day and the night. *Tuus est dies et tua est nox.*

At the first glance, childhood, youth, and middle life seem to have all sorts of advantages over old age; but, like the phantasmagoria of wealth and rank, these disappear on a nearer view. Childhood of course has the advantage in time; but it knows not what precious germs it bears within, what blessings are by it attainable. It is not in the secret of its own advantages, and has no realization of its own blessedness. It understands not the why and wherefore of its enforced actions, knows nothing of ends, or of means in their relation to ends. It submits to reason as to force. Its joys are keen; but so are its sorrows. It is gay and free from care; but it is never happy.

The old man *knows;* and it is a great thing to know! And to have seen, through a long life, *God always right;* to be able to declare one's self perfectly "content [1] with him," and to admire the universal justification of his law; to have measured the nothingness of what we are leaving, weighed our own dust, and had a sure glimpse of the good that awaits us, — is not this also something?

II.

The old man is the pontiff of the past; nor does this prevent him from being the seer of the future. The clergyman represents the priesthood of eternity; the old man that of time. In him, experience delivers oracles and prophecies; and repeatedly, in those imperfect states of society where the offices of priest and magistrate are combined, it has rested with the *ancients* of the people to maintain and perpetuate the beneficent and saving conceptions of right and of eternity.

The aged are Christ's poor: their wrinkles are their rags; they warm themselves in the sunbeams; they beg their daily bread.

The gods ordained the blindness of Tiresias, that he might live more with themselves than with men. Old age is a species of blindness with reference to the outward world. It would seem as if the eye

---

[1] Bourdaloue.

grew dim and the ear less sensitive to earthly sounds, that the contemplation might be more profound and the attention more fully given to the voice within. God succeeds to all the relinquished desires and suppressed transports of the old, and opens to them more and more of the interior life.

The silence which pervades the being renders the slightest sound audible. The eye is quick and practised; for experience is a second sight, showing what shall be in what has been.

The old man is like a sentinel on the outpost of life. Sleep flies his eyelids. The watch he keeps is solemn as a knight's vigil.

With singular goodness, God has rendered a disposition to sleeplessness nearly universal with the old. Life is worth more than sleep. God would fain multiply the attainments of the aged; and, since time presses, He gives them an increasing share in that *watchfulness* which the Scripture places between prayer and alms. "Watch and pray," saith our Lord. This means of sanctification is easy to the old, but little suited to the young.

"Youth is the loveliest flower on earth," says an old Breton song.[1] Old age, let me add, is the most savory fruit.

The ripe fruit is sweeter than the green.

---

[1] See the "Chants Populaires de la Bretagne," translated by Count de la Villemarqué, of the Institute. Vol. ii. p. 391.

Misfortune discovers to youth the nothingness of life; it reveals to age the happiness of heaven.

The coldest Christians consecrate the morning and the evening to God. So infancy and old age are especially under his patronage.

The old man, like the husbandman of St. James, "waiteth for the precious fruit of the earth, and hath patience for it, till he receive the early and the latter rain."

Thus, like the cross of Calvary, the old man is midway between heaven and earth, — held to the one by his duties,to the other by his hopes. He believes; because he has proved all things, and only the truth of the gospel has remained at the bottom of the crucible.

Old age is life on its holy Saturday, — the eve of the glorious resurrection, — the morrow of all the distractions of earth and the sufferings of the cross.

The God of eternity, who comprehends all times in one, seems to have willed that the three grand divisions of time should exist and be represented simultaneously in creation. Age is the past, infancy the future, youth the present. Experience — a virtue drawn from the past — has to clarify youth's force of conception and vigor of action.

Old age, with its wisdom, is to the peremptory and positive notions of youth what tradition is to written doctrine.

Age no longer moulds the bronze or "rough-hews" the marble; but it perfects, it finishes, it does that patient and assiduous work, which, through life, is the justification of God's law. An aged and illustrious *savant* once said: "The more I study, and the more I observe, the less I can explain," a remark full of philosophy in the mouth of a philosopher, but incomprehensible in that of a Christian. Each day, the Christian comprehends better the destiny which God has appointed him, and the reason of the weights with which he has charged it.

III.

By reason of sin, old age is the twilight of death, but God can extract from all the elements of our fallen nature harmonies full of beauty. He employs the old, — the ancients, — to bear witness to his past mercies, among the rising generations.

Old age is not one of the beauties of creation, but it is one of its harmonies. The law of contrasts is one of the laws of beauty. Under the conditions of our climate, shadow gives light its worth; sternness enhances mildness; solemnity, splendor. Varying proportions of size support and subserve one another. Different flavors give zest to one another. Nothing could vanish from the earth without leaving a void. Hierarchy — even in age — is one of God's beautiful and harmonious thoughts, and he loses no opportunity of illustrating it in his works.

God deigns to provide by his care for all that has served himself or his purposes. This old age — though one of the effects of the fall — is far from expressing punishment alone; and the most diverse of evils have their compensations. Side by side with infirmities and privations, we have fewer occasions of strife, deep and strong consolations, secrets of infinite tenderness, and a thousand revelations from the Husband[1] of our souls, which have rendered for many a one the end of life far sweeter than its beginning.

Nothing gives rise to so many contradictions in the human mind as old age. It is a phantom in which youth has no faith; a scarecrow to virile complacency. Yet no sooner have we attained the apogee of life, — no sooner have we taken our first downward step upon the opposite slope, than we cease, at heart, to dread old age, but anticipate it, all of us, and make the best terms possible with its inconveniences.

In the pride of its strength, youth claims long life as a right, and rejects the idea of growing old. Strange to say, it is not horror that old age excites: it is contempt. Does the feeling attach to old age itself, or to the manner of growing old? "In our day," said M. de Chateaubriand, "people are old, but they are no longer venerable." This remark,

---

[1] "Thy Maker is thy husband."— IsAIAH lxiv. 5.

perhaps, contains the whole secret of the slight respect of youth for age.

When I say that youth does not believe in age for itself, I have no fear of exaggerating. Positively, its treats the idea as a superstition, and passes it by with disdain; does it not even the honor of treating it as a necessary evil, and accepting it as it accepts death. It promises itself some escape, and glories in being unwilling to prolong life at the price of so much ignominy. But this does not last long. Time slips away, the attention is given to other things, youth loses itself in mature life, and soon gray hairs are announcing the approach of the great hoar-frost. And now we no longer think of old age as a thing to be shunned, but begin, by way of neutralizing its severity, to parley with it, to question it; even admitting that, after all, there may be some advantage to be derived therefrom. We devour our years somewhat as a schoolboy does the cherries in his basket, — taking first the finest, then the good, then the tolerable, and finally enjoying those which we at first refused.

Why should not old age be the ninth book of the sibyl, for which we pay the price of the nine, and which is worth them all?

Time is the shower of Danaë. Each drop is golden.

Youth lives in abundance with respect to time; but what is wealth whose value we do not know, and which we lavish without forethought and without regret? Old age teaches the value of time, and apprises us that our most precious treasure is its raw material. The man who avails most is he who best employs his time; the wisest, he who turns it to the greatest advantage. Time is the representative of all moral, intellectual, and even spiritual worth. The wealthiest man is he whose wide horizon is bounded by God. It is the old man, above all, who can say with Young, in his admirable verse, "Time is eternity, — pregnant with all eternity can give."

Knowing the value of time, we aspire to save and employ it. In our eagerness to improve the moments, the soul outstrips the organs, and we are like that Ariadne of Dannecker,[1] who plainly moves faster than the panther that bears her. On the one hand, her desire springs to the pursuit of Theseus; on the other, she must needs submit to the pace of the beast she rides, her only means of rapid locomotion. It is a fine image of old age, — of the ardent soul which hurries onward, straining for the goal, but which, being dependent on matter for the means of progress here below, is hindered by those very means. How should it not travel faster than the poor body, — a panting panther shorn of its strength and agility? It is the heart that supplies swiftness. Old

---

[1] The masterpiece of the sculptor Dannecker, in the gallery of M. Bethmann, at Frankfort.

age is seen to be great at heart, despite all its signs of weakness.

IV.

As far as the natural man is concerned, youth has the advantage in every respect; even in moral qualities. Thus, generosity, self-devotion, noble and disinterested sentiments, belong eminently to youth. If the love of God does not keep the heart warm, the action of time and contact with men tend only too surely to relax and chill its generous transports. Youth is a sort of temporary divinity; impressing on its creatures brilliant virtues, that last during its own stay. For the mind and the character, there is a *beauté du diable*, — a charm of freshness, spontaneity, and bloom, which supplies the place of regular beauty and solid qualities. With the spiritual man it is not so. He is born later, and under harder conditions, which ordain that he shall be helped by his very hindrances. While youth is but a vehicle for the natural man, age profits by every trial. The same force is differently directed. That which, when young, we did for ourselves, when old we do for God. Then, all is purified and nothing weakened. It is the same flame; but subtler, more vivid, because nourished by rarer elements.

For the natural man, I must repeat, youth is the best, perhaps the only good, time. Its absence of calculation, the fulness and spontaneousness of its good actions, its easier forgiven faults, lift it above that age which abstains from certain vices, indeed, but shrinks from many a good work. Nature, then, has done every thing for youth; but religion is diametrically opposed to nature, and, by its divine counterpoises, more than restores the equilibrium between the seasons of life. And so, for the freshness, the grace, the splendor of natural qualities, it substitutes the massiveness, the height, the worth of virtues; like the drop of wax, which, as it condenses, gains in solidity what it loses in brightness. The ship of youth crowds sail; but, if the wind forsakes it, the canvas hangs motionless, awaiting a friendly breath; and too often illusions are summoned to its aid: while the old man never ceases, though tired, to wield the oar and guide the helm.

The poor ship of age is battered. Once it strove with a storm of flowers, but now with a storm of snow. Its keel has grazed so often! Its sails are torn. Its helm only still resists the waves.

v.

If truth is all-important; if reality has its resources as well as its sorrows, and a strength that compensates for lost illusions, — then advanced age is superior to the epoch of falsehood and optical delusions. It is less exacting with regard to life; for it takes it at a lower rate, and so is more apt to be satisfied. "Happiness is something which we attain most easily when we have renounced it," says Mme. de Staël.

In such a mood as this, old age generally finds us. Suffer as we may, from the loss of illusions, I am unable to comprehend how he who is honored by the possession of truth can ever regret them.

Old age is the last word of truth on this earth, — the realization of all which is revealed to us concerning the nothingness of its prosperities, and of all which is not connected, nearly or remotely, with the eternal promises. It declares the wisdom of the divine teachings, and that God alone is all. Old age is truly the period of the grand council, the mere sight of which pleads and invites to the right way.

VI.

Christianity apart, I admit that the old man —

"De son âge a tout le malheur."

But why consider any season of life without reference to the thought that embraces them all? God has willed that we should find many things established by himself; but, when we depart from his order, on what recompense or indemnification can we rely? What right could we offset against the indefeasible right we disregard?

Christianity came into the world to aid weakness of every kind. It has taught us to respect childhood, which it called to its embrace. Hitherto, woman had been but the slave of man. Christianity made her his companion, and, as a crowning grace, placed her under the sheltering care of him to whose rank she was raised. Old age is despoiled by nature and the world alike. Antiquity merely amused it with outward marks of respect. Its wisdom and experience were consulted, but its individual life was over, its future destroyed, its gaze fixed on the past, its sole possession the blessings that were slipping from its grasp. Christianity has done more for old age than for any other period of life; for it shows how to face an inglorious death without shrinking. Not merely has courage in view of death no glory for the old man, who seems to be forsaken by life rather than to quit it; but virtue in him seems so entirely the necessary fruit of experience and satiety, that there appears to be no merit in its practice. Nevertheless, this season has its special and often inextricable difficulties. God sees the worth which is encouraged by no human approbation, and the All-seeing Eye watches the old man as closely as the young.

All conditions and all ages have been studied from the Christian point of view; except, perhaps, old age. And let no one offer, as an excuse, that it is a stranger to the affections that vivify life, and has lost its warmth and its sap. Truly, it breathes an air less bright and burning than of yore: its thermometer is placed in the shade, but its warmth is that of the atmosphere at large, not that of the sun blazing down on a single point.

Christianity has been applied as a palliative to all ills; but there is one on which its transforming power has very seldom been tried; and that is old age. Alms-houses have been built for the old, and pains taken to provide them shelter and lodging; but some effort is also needed to reconcile them to their condition, and reveal to them its resources.

Would God have left without consolation precisely the last stage of the journey we are making to his home? God prolongs our life, and fills it with bitterness. What ground of perfect trust is here! Only that which is to be used is purified; only the iron which is to be wrought is beaten; only the wound which we would heal is probed.

Life grows darker as we go on, till only one pure light is left shining on it; and that is faith. Old age, like solitude and sorrow, has its revelations.

There is a Scripture word which saith, "*Quand tu auras fini, tu commenceras.*" Toward the close of our career, many an idea and word of wisdom, which previously had been but an empty sound, receives a soul, and is informed with unguessed life. How beautiful and grand a thing it is, to grow old under the eyes of God! The reason why we fear old age so much, is because we separate it from him. Mine has outlived its dreams; but, if it had them still, rest would be the least seductive of them all. Peace? Yes; but not rest. There is none in this world; nor should there be. In Armand's last illness, some one urged him to rest. "Rest!" replied the poor dying creature; "I shall have all eternity for that."

Of course, our activity changes its nature, and its sphere is circumscribed. The decline of our bodily strength necessarily retards our steps; but it draws its principle from the soul and its instincts, and its aims remain unchanged. The notes are the same, only struck a few octaves lower. But I understand well — and better and better each day — that a struggle is inaugurated between the persistent will and the failing vitality; and I must confess that, of all the vagaries of the Roman emperors, the most comprehensible to me is that of the emperor who determined to die standing.

VII.

It is evident that the epoch of life into which are crowded the greatest number of trials is old age. The universal feeling proves it. "People are no longer happy at our age," said Louis XIV. to Marshal Villeroy. After the raising of the siege of Metz, the same thought was expressed by Charles V.; and it was he, too, who made that remark, as brilliant as it was profound: "Fortune loves only the young."

Yet, dull as they are, the days of advanced life are precious. Whether we consider them as days of expiation, or days of grace, their place is among the most spiritual of God's providences. Just as, in those unlooked-for events which are generally attributed to chance, we see God's hand all the plainer for being less sensible of human action, — so these divinely prolonged years are more necessary the more useless they appear. It is the hour in which the chrysalis awakes. The new life it is to assume within leaves the outside barer than ever of beauty and of life.

Yes, save in the exceptional cases of a few predestined individuals, old age is a blessing; for, who would dare say with Tobit, "It is profitable for me to die, rather than to live"? Each day accorded to the old man is, not a reprieve, — a delay sterile if not agonizing, — but a useful season in which he may modify or atone for the sins of the past, diminish, and perhaps liquidate, his debt, move and soften his judge, and convert his sentence into an acquittal.

And what a benediction is a Christian old age! How many developments it presents, unattainable either by youth or by maturity! This halt at the journey's end permits the traveller to wipe the sweat from his brow, and to shake off the dust that soils him, before entering his Father's festal hall. "Upborne by supernatural power, he quits the last summits he had climbed. His look has been upward; and he sees, face to face. He aspired to reunion; and reunion is effected."[1] He despises not

---

[1] Du Mariage au Point de Vue Chrétien. By Mme. de Gasparin. Vol. iii. p. 178.

the world nor the goods that he abandons; but he sees them from another hemisphere, and their proportions are changed.

All is sad for the old man; but may we not discover, in this very absence of sweet and pleasing impressions, the hidden sense, — the key to the riddle, — the meaning of the moment of life the sphinx allows us?

"Il n'a plus en mourant à perdre que la vie."

He who penned this verse hardly suspected to what order of truth its melancholy beauty belongs. Sad state indeed from the human point of view, for him who, living on external goods alone, outlives himself necessarily if these are taken away. But, on the other hand, do we not really take possession of the best part of ourselves when all those things which crushed and weighed us down have successively disappeared? Is there no dignity in the renunciation — profoundly submissive, if not voluntary — of all which flattered cupidity or ambition, — in the celestial peace which consoles us a thousand-fold for the loss of happiness, which plants the smile upon our lips, and removes the lightest cloud from the brow? No: life has not conquered the old man: it is he who rises superior to life.

VIII.

From a worldly point of view, old age is a misfortune; and, like all misfortunes, should be borne with dignity. It asks a staff, but not a crutch. Humanly speaking, old age is a disgrace; for a certain sense of shame undoubtedly accompanies it. It has a kind of inferiority, for it is timid. According to the world, it is a series of degradations. Time is its direct and natural enemy; and those who acknowledge the supreme authority of time become the executors of its judgment against age. In God, on the contrary, time is no more; and, since eternity has already begun for old age, its last foe is slain. Age would indeed be humiliating if, as the body decays, the soul did not gain in dignity; but, as princes rise in rank as they approach the throne, so the old man mounts the steps of eternity by successive promotions.

It has been remarked, with great justice, that morality in individuals is grander, in proportion as they are able to sacrifice the present to the future. Thus, the sensualist, blinded by passion, is carried away by the impulse of the moment. He yields to his fierce appetites as thoughtlessly as the Caribbean, who abandons his couch in the morning without reflecting that he will need it at night; while the moral man forms and develops his plans, and, by his own laborious effort, attains the proposed end.

When the end is worthy, the enlightened man makes no account of time. He can trade on long credit; and, sometimes, without even knowing that he is eternal, he can be patient.

When we see a man undertaking a work whose accomplishment he will not witness, are we not touched by such devotion to the well-being of posterity?

When a young man even plants an oaken forest, or lays the first stone of an edifice which will be generations in building, is it not affecting to think of his self-sacrifice for those whom he knows not, and who will never know him? Ah, well! the old man's life is well-nigh filled with such disinterested deeds. All his beginnings are acorns, and of none of his hopes will he see the full-grown oak. He may finish what he begins, but others will enjoy it.

The world enters with marvellous readiness into this view of the old man, and assumes the responsibility of all its consequences; and so, acts of which the world makes no account, acquire, in the eyes of God, the magnanimity and purity of intention which make them pleasing to Him.

And so it is that, entering unconsciously into the designs of Providence, the world hastens the perfection of the aged by purifying their virtue from all human leaven, and leaving undiminished the reward that awaits them. Well does the gospel say that man is not rewarded twice. The virtues formed, developed, and practised under the eyes of God alone, in the secrecy of solitude, rank next in merit to those deeds of the right hand which the left hand knoweth not. Human observation and eulogium have not tarnished them, and none of their virtue is wasted.

To reap the full fruit of the good deeds we have done is rarer than we think; and to the observation and flattery of the world is probably due nearly all the waste they must necessarily undergo.

The uninterrupted practice of virtue at this age becomes, in reference to the world, something resembling what is called, in the interior life, the state of pure faith, — wherein the soul, smitten with barrenness, finds no consolation in its belief. We but vegetate in the eyes of the world which tolerates us, as though we were of the nature of that idol of which the prophet spoke, — without eyes, mouth, ears, or voice: a condition as wonderful as the death we die, that we may henceforth live to God; live silent and watchful, hearing only his words, partaking only of his spirit.

IX.

An ingenious writer has said that "fifty is the youth of old age. It is a brief youth." Local ravages soon begin, and are promptly followed by general decrepitude. The charity of the world dares not say, with the American savage, that the aged must be slain; but, while leaving them alive, it ceases greatly to regard them. If they retain the dignity suited to their years, people avoid them for fear of imposing constraint or inconvenience upon themselves. If they condescend voluntarily to renounce themselves, and wear another uniform, contempt and ridicule await them. Their exterior is scanned with ill-natured curiosity. They are pronounced to have either too much or too little self-respect. Do they endeavor to —

"Réparer des ans l'irréparable outrage,"

the world laughs in its sleeve, at their futile efforts. If, on the contrary, there are any signs of carelessness, the world, indignant at all lack of consideration for itself, protests against the cynicism of these gray hairs and toothless gums; this ugliness, in short, enhanced to the last degree. "After all," 'tis said, "society deserves some respect, and if people appear therein it must be on certain conditions."

If you would appreciate the worth of an aged person, notice how many times old age is adduced as a plea in bar. Is the old man pious? You will be told that it is a makeshift. Does he strive to be burdensome to none, and to show that he is easy to please? 'Tis because his heart has grown old like his body, rest has become his chief good, and his disinterestedness is only indifference. Does a sacred charm invite him to solitude? He has merely calculated the best means of concealing his regret for lost privileges, and his envy of those whom he sees in possession around him. Are the bounties of the old man large? What merit have they since he is insensible to privation, and only gives what he is soon to leave; besides, what use is there in having a *sou* after sixty? If he is mild, it is because the blood in his veins is iced; if he is patient in sickness, it is but rational to remember the conditions of his age; if he is resigned to death, has he not lived long? In short, he has not a single virtue, but the world must needs question it.

I admit that there is some truth in these accusations, and therefore something avoidable; for a just reproach almost always implies the capability of amendment. But the exquisite tact which enables one to choose his way amid impediments is rare, — rare as all perfection, and in one way or another there is always something for the critic to lay hold of.

X.

What is true of old men is yet truer of old women. Of all human beings, they have the least credit. The old woman, as the world goes, is something that does not even have, like the old man, a name in the elevated style. She is such rubbish that even those who would do her honor must avoid her name, and have recourse to a circumlocution.

There is no sadder sight than that of an aged woman, stripped of the consideration and respect that belong to the dignity of a serious life. The poor old woman, and her trial begins early, is a being who has positively no place beneath the sun. Even by the domestic hearth, her right is precarious and disputed; and, outside of actual life, her portion is no better.

She is, with a few rare exceptions, excluded from the creations of the artist and the poet; and the thought of her hardly ever occurs to the moralist, who leaves her to work out her own salvation as best she may. Our priests themselves, many of them starting, it may be, from the natural point of view, are too much in the habit of regarding even old men only as persons whose end is at hand. The chrysalis makes them forget the butterfly. But who cares for an old woman after her life has ceased to be scandalous? Who allows her progress in virtue? Who comes to her aid in spiritual ways? Men are of some account, even in advanced years. We are proud of a conquest if that conquest be a man, and take good care to preserve it; but it is far otherwise with women, whose pettiness and chatter, doubtless, furnish occasions against them. Are we not sure of retaining these; and who is not rendered cold and careless by security? Yes, often the priest himself, bound to the service of weakness and infirmity; the priest, of all other men, turns his back upon the aged woman, or passes her by. His is the arm and mind of youth, when he would contend with youth or strengthen it in combat. Ripe age, as a regnant, governing force, has his sympathies, and his good will. He has zeal for the child, encouragement for the adult, reverence for the old man. For the old woman, what has he but neglect or abandonment? And, however slight her attempt at virtue, he feels as sure of her salvation as of the health of those uninteresting persons who are always well. But is not a soul a soul to whatever body bound? Have we any rule for the transports of religious emotion? Are not people converted at all ages; and is conversion ever complete till God has obtained all his will?

Let an aged woman obliterate herself; let her remind the world of her existence only by the favors and pleasures she bestows on others; and the world graciously allows her to live, — recognizes her for an inoffensive being, and all goes smoothly.

The single social virtue of the old woman — the virtue which is exactly in keeping with the part she plays in the world — is self-abnegation. In her it is at once an obligatory virtue and a spontaneous grace. The uselessness to which society, as well as nature, condemns her, is a sure index of providential design. Let the old woman have every imaginable virtue, but all in self-denial. She must die to herself sincerely and entirely; the public would be as hard to deceive as God himself in this respect. Would she examine or correct herself in any one point, prompt and conspicuous justice is executed on her at once. The essence of her virtue is the being useful to those who come in contact with her; her kindness is a universal balm; her wise prudence is security; her humble sweetness is often the peace of the house where she dwells; her generosity, the wealth of those about her. Self-renunciation — so fruitful in a man — has, in the case of a woman, results which are less lofty, doubtless, but neither less appreciable nor less generally appreciated; and so the old woman becomes convenient, which is, just now, no despicable quality. She is one who requires nothing, and gives all; who is of no more account than if she were absent, and who is disposed of as if she were always present; whom we do not feel bound to seek, but whom we are always sure of finding; and, on the whole, a rather good piece of furniture.

XI.

It is well for old age to suffer, — it is, in fact, its normal condition, — but it must not weep: tears solace youth alone. When they flow over the wrinkles of age, sympathy is no longer by to wipe them away, nor glowing love to dry these last autumnal dews.

"When thou wast young," said our Lord to St. Peter, "thou girdedst thyself, and walkedst whither thou wouldst; but when thou shalt be old, thou shalt stretch forth thy hand, and another shall gird thee, and carry thee whither thou wouldst not." The old are clogged and fettered on every side. Dependence and a hard servitude weigh heavily on their enfeebled organs. But, as their chains grow heavier and are more closely riveted, as their supports fail and their ties are silently loosened, what new liberties break their shells and try their wings! What unchecked aspirations, what a sense of deliverance, what freedom of motion through the enlarged space! Is not the aged Christian the freest of Jesus Christ's freemen? What is external dependence compared to the perfect liberty within?

This perfect liberty of the old man —

"Lui permet la franchise, attribut des vieux ans."

This frankness may rise even to boldness; for, while redoubling its care and caution for others, old age makes free use of absolute independence for itself. Youth has present, living interests to care for, and a long future unfolding before it; but age can brave all with a moral good in view. The pearl of great price is always before the eyes of the aged. They would seek it in the depths of the sea.

In youth, we need external help in all matters pertaining to salvation. In age, every thing conduces to it; and that which was against us is for us. And so those faults and propensities, which were but ill-directed forces, are all turned to good account in the new application which is made of them, and from the moment when God takes them into his own hands.

How well it is, if God prolongs life, to have its too external activities interrupted; and to employ it in a higher, a deeper, a more spiritual service! The influence exerted upon ourselves and others loses nothing of its power thereby; but, if its radius is shorter, its strength is more concentrated; the good we effect changes its sphere, but is not abated; and nothing, it seems to me, is so reasonable as a transition which puts in more direct communication our means and end of action. Old age is a kind of novitiate in spirituality. The outside world is slipping away, — it rests less upon itself; it is becoming less fit to subserve material interests, but the others remain. Old age is the novitiate of death, — but of that death, pregnant with life, which is promised to the Christian. The novitiate partakes of the character of the succeeding state; and death, which is the veil of immortality on this side the solemn passage, is tinged by the fires that are to come.

People are always talking of the darkness of the grave. I am far more impressed by the beams that issue from it. Old age is on the best plane to receive them. Death is the justification of all the Christian's ways; the conclusive reason for all his sacrifices; that touch of the great Master that completes the picture.

XII.

One great cause of regret for old age is, that our Lord has not sanctified this period of life by passing through it. It is the sole age to which he has not bequeathed his example. The teachings of his childhood, silent though they be, are none the less instructive. Still the gospel develops them but slightly. Only his middle life is, as one may say, in light; as if to teach us that, as children, we must hasten to become men, and, later, to become saints.

XIII.

Old age is the majestic and imposing dome of human life. God makes it the sanctuary of all wisdom and justice; the tabernacle of the purest virtues. Experience has taught the old man all things; and his personal endeavors have reduced his acquirements to that simple state, — that perfect unity, — where each conviction has its proof and counter-proof. His are the treasures of tradition, and those of acquired knowledge, — ancient lore and modern facts, in their order, practical truth, and eternal verity, the relative and the absolute, — that which helps our conduct in this world, and that which leads us to another. If death were only the blossoming of life, — the sublime flower of that plant whose spreading roots underlie the earth, — if, as saith the apostle, death merely clothed us with immortality: old age would be the apogee of life, — its culminating point, its epoch of wealth and power. But it must not be forgotten that death is the wages of sin; and, as such, it causes the weight of our condemnation to fall heavily upon old age. Old age is the term of grace — sometimes a little protracted — when all accounts must be audited, all allowances confirmed, and when the invisible Creditor exacts his dues. Of all the seasons of life, old age is that in which the sentence with which man is weighted is most keenly felt. The forecast shadow of death overspreads the close of life. But death has been redeemed, like all things else. Old age is the central point. Night is on one side, and dawn on the other. Ransomed death permits a passage to the beams of the true life, and our last twilights are nearer than any others to the eternal light.

We can understand why pagan antiquity should have been as little able as scepticism itself to grasp these changeful glimmerings of old age, — deep darkness or growing light, — according to the side from which we view them, or the point where we stand; according as we hope or deny.

Horace called death "*in æternum exilium:*" a going away into eternal exile. The Christian calls it a return to his everlasting fatherland. Here is all the difference between the two points of view.

There is, in Russia, an old and very touching custom, which our ancestors used faithfully to observe. In the hour of departure, when the preparations are complete, all seat themselves, — travellers and by-standers, — making a solemn halt, as if to collect their thoughts for the last time, before the supreme moment of separation. Is it not a striking type of old age, which is itself a halt before departure, —

"Voyageurs d'un moment aux terres étrangeres,
Consolez-vous, vous êtes immortels"!

All question of the old man's well-being becomes a question of immortality, according as the point of departure is a life which is passing away, or a life for which he is momently preparing. If the thoughts of faith are deeply impressed upon his soul, what a sight must he not see in this vanquished world, — the raw material of all the changes which have taken place within himself!

We say "declining years;" but, if heaven be our true centre, the decline of our twofold being is contemporaneous with its ascent. Soul and body are in almost perpetual contradiction. In the failing of nature, it is not merely destruction which is hastening on, but liberty and glory, — the perfection of a soul which grows ever more radiant as the spiritual principle absorbs all others. As the body sinks into decrepitude, the soul is tempered; and, by the simultaneous acceleration of these two processes, the frame returns to the dust, and the spirit to heaven. Death for the one is immortal youth for the other. David was old when he called upon the God of his youth: but it was not the God of his past whom he invoked, any more than the God of Jacob is the God of the dead. It was the God of the present to whom David appealed, — the God of that youth which he felt flourishing and blossoming in the depths of his being. For if the children of light enjoy day in the midst of night, the children of immortality keep their youth amid the snows of age.

XIV.

Old age is not denied fertility. Behold how the aged tree clothes itself with a foliage as young as that of the shrub; bearing flowers and fruit while its life lasts, whatever be the number of the years that have left their date on the bark of its aged stem. While the tree lives, it produces leafage; and, in default of fruit, yields shelter and shade. And, in the spiritual order, God has willed that man should always have the power to conceive and bring forth the new man; not miraculously, like Sarah and Elizabeth, but regularly and of right.

While all created things, our bodies included, speedily attain their last degree of development and perfection, then pause, and turn, — so to speak, — rounding the circle of their organism or their instinct, to where weakness and decadence take them back to their original state; man, on the contrary, — the human intelligence, — grows and develops unceasingly in all his faculties. He pursues an unlimited career, a perpetually ascending line of knowledge and virtue.

The error which consists in believing that the Church can have an era of decrepitude, is one with that which allows a similar failure of the immaterial principle in man. These opinions go hand in hand, because there is in both cases a question of assimilating the law which governs mind to that which governs matter.

Observe, by the way, that our celebrated prosewriters preserve their superiority till the decline of life; while our poets, save in cases of extraordinary genius, fall with the winter. Thought with the former dwells constantly on the sober realities of the Christian life: with the latter, it is but a pastime. But this playfulness demands a sensuous rapture, of which the old have ceased to be capable; and 'tis a glorious impotence, for which they should not grieve. What laments over bright days gone we find in the votaries of the Muses! What contempt of youth in Bossuet! The great bishop dates life only by white hairs.[1]

Yet the true poets, like the great artists, have scarcely any childhood, and no old age.

XV.

It is said that old age freezes the activity of man in the performance of spiritual duty. What matters this, O my God! if thou dost provide therefor? Already hath the gospel taught us, that, before thy tribunal, there is neither Greek, Barbarian, nor Scythian. Even so, its divine spirit further instructs us that, in thy eyes, souls have neither age nor sex. I know it: faith, like virtue, is independent of the number of one's years; yet who believes that the im-

---

[1] Moreau, "Considérations sur la Vraie Doctrine." 1844. 8vo. pp. 198, 199.

mediate approach of the inevitable end has not, after all, a significance and an effect peculiar to itself? The venerable Abbé Desjardins said, two or three years before his death, that it was barely eighteen months since he first saw the things of this world in their true light relative to those of eternity. The approach of the formidable moment perfected his intellect; and, from being a pious, learned, and always irreproachable Christian, he became a saint.

"O faces of the saints; sweet and firm lips, accustomed to name the name of God, and to kiss the cross of his Son; dear glances, which discern a brother in the poorest creature; hairs blanched by meditations on eternity, sacred colors of the soul shining in age and death, — blessed are they who have seen you; more blessed they who have understood, and who have received from your transfigured contours lessons of wisdom and immortality."[1]

XVI.

Has aught in nature been utterly disinherited? When was God known wholly to abandon the work of his hands? Has not winter its beauties? Do not its rigors set off its charms? In our harsh climate is not the sky deep and blue? Does not the sun cover the hoar-frost with diamonds, and draw sparkles from the jewelled snow? Have we not, in stern

---

[1] Father Lacordaire, 48th Sermon.

winter, by way of contrast to the roaring storm and the icy cold without, the gathering about the fireside, where the covered fire retains a warmth amid the ashes, which fitly symbolizes the constant temperate heat of the old man's heart, — a mild, soft glow, — ever the same amid all the vagaries and devastations of the changeful human seasons?

In my long winter journeys, I have often been struck by remarkable effects of form and light, attesting that nature no more than man undergoes that passive condition of anticipated death to which the world would fain condemn old age. Ah! in the works of God, and in our hearts, there is always life and power enough for love and blessing; always space for us to cry with the prophets, —

"O ye fire and heat, bless ye the Lord! O ye winter and summer, bless ye the Lord! O ye dews and storms of snow, bless ye the Lord! O ye ice and cold, bless ye the Lord! O ye frost and snow, bless ye the Lord! O ye nights and days, bless ye the Lord!"[1]

"Bless ye the Lord, all ye servants of the Lord, which by night stand in the house of the Lord!"

"Lift up your hands in the sanctuary, and bless the Lord."[2]

Old age is the night of life, and night the old age

---

[1] The Song of the Three Holy Children, chap. v. 44–50.
[2] Ps. cxxxiv.

of the day; yet is the night full of magnificence, and, for many, more brilliant than the day. With many, night is the place for thought; as God is the place of the soul, and space that of the body. There reflection holds audience, and meditation seeks an asylum. There it is that we best hear and comprehend that silence which is, in the words of Philo, the voice of God. To old age has been accorded the nearest and plainest manifestation of God, as it has been given to the night to be the witness of Christ's birth and resurrection; shining nights, which have been honored by the name of blessed.

Infinite are the analogies between age and night! We must contemplate the one in God, as we must study the other in the heavens. Think whether there are seasons for the dear stars in the firmament; then look at the night of age. That, too, is sown with stars; and the old man, like the sky, has naught to do with seasons. The changeful world sways and tosses at his feet, but the impassibility of the firmament is already his. Let him retire into the realm of his own pious thoughts. He has room enough there; and, whether winter or summer smite the lower regions, the upper air is always blue, and every diamond is a world.

Sometimes, in the long polar nights, there comes a glimmer like that of dawn, which, for a moment, dispels the shadows; so, in the night of advanced age, instinctive illuminations greet the gaze, which seem to belong to a coming day. The night hours have been good to me; and it is rare, indeed, that these beloved companions fail to bring me a blessing in the guise of some holy thought or emotion.

"Day is for man," an old writer has said, "and night is for the gods." Yes: the day, with its noise and activity, belongs to man and his affairs, — as do youth, and the strength of manhood; while the night, with its silence and meditation, is God's, — like age, wherein the thought of heaven predominates over all the interests of life. Is not this period like the rest which follows the last hour of daylight, — the rest which comes when our duties are all done? And are not the last years of the old man's life, which correspond to these late hours, peculiarly his own, more so than any other? Has he not discharged all his debts, — this veteran of the earth, — and, it may be, in the words of the psalmist, "paid that which he owed not." What remains is his own, — all his own. And this, his possession, what is it but God?

"The Lord commandeth his loving-kindness in the day-time, and our songs of thanksgiving in the night."[1]

The higher we mount, the later comes the night. Age is the hill "whence cometh our help." When all around is folded and lost in shadow, that peak,

---

[1] Ps. xliii.

visited by the sunbeams, shines with the gathered brightness of a long life, and shows from afar like a watch-tower.

What was Anna, the daughter of Phanuel, but a lamp burning in the temple? And does not the gospel teach us, by the example of this saintly widow, that age may pass its night without ever quitting the temple; serving God in fasting and prayer, — fasting from all human joys, unceasing prayer to him for whose coming it waits?[1]

What is it to wait for God on the strength of his word, but to taste at once the charm of mystery and the great joy of certainty; to discern across a golden twilight the brightness of the uncreated light; to have, at the same time, the rapture of learning and knowing; to collect our thoughts for happiness; to prepare ourselves for joy; to call, and feel that we are answered?

"If any man hear my voice, and open the door, I will come in with him and sup with him, and he with me."[2] Happy old age! It is for supper, and not for a mid-day feast, where noise and tumult reign; it is to *sup* with us that our Lord will come: at the close of the dull, weary, toilsome day; at the hour of long, sweet, friendly talks, when intimacy grows deepest, and confidence flows with a full stream; at night-fall, when hearts approach and

---

[1] Luke ii. 4. [2] Rev. xi. 20.

mingle, and think of naught save how to bless and sanctify the sleep which is to follow.

I collect myself, O my God! at the close of life, as at the close of day, and bring to thee my thoughts and my love. The last thoughts of a heart that loves thee, are like those last, deepest, ruddiest rays of the setting sun. Thou hast willed, O my God! that life should be beautiful even to the end. Make me to grow and keep my green, and climb like the plant which lifts its head to thee for the last time before it drops its seed and dies.

NUNC DIMITTIS.

A STEEPER slope, a stronger impulse, hurry me to the tomb. Each hour, as it passes, strips me of something, and carries me a few steps farther down. The grains of dust at the bottom of the clepsydra are few; and I count them without terror. How imposing are these remaining years of ours, — these years which may be but a day! The eve of any great day has a character of solemnity, and the greatest of all dawns in eternity.

Nunc dimittis. Now lettest thou thy servant depart in peace, O Lord! His load is lightened. The weakest of thy angels could carry it under his wing. His swelling pride is humbled. The *ego* has lost its substance. The world has withdrawn its stupid favors. The weight of sin has been removed by forgiveness and tears; and beneath thy light and easy yoke all his limbs move freely.

CHRISTIANITY,

PROGRESS, AND CIVILIZATION.

IF man were not a perpetual recipient; if he had created, discovered, or chanced upon aught that he possesses; if all germs were native within him, and brought to light by some unassisted creative virtue of his own, — I could understand how, in consequence of such a beginning, so unlike his actual origin, it would be impossible for him ever to pause or to end. On this hypothesis, the very fact that he had grasped primary truths would make it inevitable that the infinite order to which they belong should reveal to him its inexhaustible treasures.

But in reality it is not so. By the association of matter with the undying soul, human power and activity have been circumscribed on every side. God has selected, from the infinite store-house of his wisdom, certain notions which he has made the patrimony and common groundwork of humanity; he has limited their number, so to speak, as he has that of colors and sounds. All the rest of the eternal

Father's domain is inaccessible to man. He explores only the sphere in which he is shut up; his exploits are confined to a given corner of the earth; for to him, as to the ocean, have been set bounds that he cannot pass over. Do we say, then, that time has been doomed to impotence, and man to inaction?

No. Time presides over the successive development and gradual progress of masses, but its years and its ages are alike powerless to make the human species attain its culminating point of intellectual or moral grandeur. What time necessarily perfects, are methods and classifications. What it creates are instruments, and this is quite glory enough. Look at letters, science, and philosophy!

Disputes have sometimes been raised about the comparative literary eminence of the ancients and the moderns. If we are to believe Fontenelle, for example, in his famous polemic against his adversary Lamotte, chronology suffices to mark the advance of the human mind. Given, the numbers of any two centuries, and we know at once which surpasses the other. No doubt the general level of science or human attainment rises, like the soil of our cities, by the simple action of time; but has the gifted man of our day more talent than the gifted man of a thousand years ago? Do we reckon many *savans* in our academies of Paris, London, or Berlin, who transcend the proportions of Pythagoras, Plato, or

Aristotle? — many architects who can outdo the Parthenon, many sculptors who eclipse Phidias or Praxiteles?

It is from the hands of the Creator that genius issues, full-armed like Minerva, without regard to date. Great men are but a result of the divine absolutism. Without revelation, — which came to apprise us of a heaven which, alas! we know not how to conquer nor even to desire, — what change could have been wrought in human destiny by the unassisted act of man?

The Christian is often confronted with the progress and the blessings attributed to the Reformation of the sixteenth, and the philosophy of the eighteenth, centuries. Now, in my opinion, what Christians should dare acknowledge to themselves, and reply to others, is this:

Yes: in the long-run there have been few more severe and humiliating punishments inflicted upon Christians than the collective events which were consummated under the name of reform, and which all arose from hatred or contempt of the Catholics.

A second test, less rigorous in its character, though equally accusatory, is the philosophy of the eighteenth century, a period during which the enemies of Christianity were left to deduce the corollary of those social truths, strongly entrenched, like truths of every sort, in the heart of the Church. The humanitarian theories of the last century made an outlet for a part only of what was latent in Christianity, and the philosophers did but attempt to extend to society what had hitherto been applied exclusively to the individual. They endeavored to enlarge the circle, and widen the application of the precept; but, in reality, every truth they ever promulgated was drawn from the fount of Christianity, and bore the mark of its spirit. But how was it that Christian society allowed itself to be outstripped by those who, at the same time, were stabbing the breast that had nourished them? What shall we say of those heedless and ungrateful sons who leave their father's estate to be pillaged by those who offer him insult? Let us be generous and indulgent to our enemies; but to the brothers whom we respect and cherish, our severity is due. Do not the faults of the Catholics touch us far more nearly than the heinous injustice of their foes? In reform and encyclopedist philosophy, therefore, for how much do the laxity and the abuses which induced them count?

The philosophers, on the other hand, cannot deny the identity of their maxims with the spirit of Christianity. What they took or gave for original views were generally only deductions from principles deposited in their hearts by early education. What they came to announce corresponded with that which it has ever been the mission of Christianity to introduce into the world, as the notes whose origin and larceny we are attempting to prove, are found upon trial to correspond with the counterparts from which they were cut off.

That the eighteenth century was animated by a sincere affection for humanity is possible; but, after all, what did it say, what did it do — or, rather, what did it desire to do — which Christianity has not comprehended within itself from all time? Christianity claims the same end and tendency, only it would have manifested a different spirit, and employed other means.

For, in short, despite those who do not shrink from employing in the meanest service the sacred majesty of the gospel, the mission of Christianity has ever been to act upon society; while holding itself utterly aloof from definite temporal contests, and taking care to impose no political regimen, properly so called. Without being unfaithful to the word of its divine Founder, — "My kingdom is not of this world," — without proposing as the immediate object of its teaching the modification of States, institutions, or laws, — bearing sway in a loftier sphere than that of the forum or the senate, — Christianity has transformed the world by transforming the conscience. It penetrates into the most secret recesses of the human heart; it strives but for the salvation of souls; yet, by a wonderful concatenation, by an indirect but infallible method, that which operates upon the individual reacts upon society at large.

Thus it is that Christianity, without affecting politics, has never failed to show itself a civilizer.

We need but to ask ourselves in what direction civilization is going or should go. It is not Christianity that will falter at this question. From whatever quarter the wind of human thought may blow, Christianity pursues its own course. It is the principle of all development; the moving force, the prime motor, in a certain sense; like steam, which serves all purposes, instead of being applicable only to a limited number of ends.

Christianity is identified with no political *régime:* its character of universality forbids this. It is the essence of progress, but it must be able to go along with all degrees of civilization. It does not wait till a people has arrived at such or such a level, but responds to all actual conditions. Indifferent to temporary accidents, it attacks the wrong principle. Wherever it encounters that, it labors to undermine it; indiscriminately aiming only at the extirpation of that evil which it came to earth to withstand. Injustice, — denial of right or contempt of humanity, wherever found, — it refers to the same source.

The social tendency of Christianity, then, is simply toward the maintenance or the establishment of God's kingdom in society, — a kingdom which is incompatible neither with a monarchy, the most perfect image of the family; nor with an oligarchy, the government of sages; nor with an aristocracy, the representative of national traditions, and the collective force of wealth and intellect; nor with a democracy, if the latter be well-disciplined and strong in its self-possession.

Transgressions of the divine law constitute not merely the sin and sorrow of the individual, but the sin and sorrow of nations. Outside of Christianity, neither prosperity nor freedom will ever be lasting. History, recording in its annals the long course of deception practised both by peoples and by kings, demonstrates the fact that, if nations and their chiefs had been more docile to the teachings of Christianity, the political condition of the world would have been far other than it is to-day.

The divine element alone can vanquish the two great powers of evil, pride and sensual desire. Pride for the mind, concupiscence for the body; these are man's two poles. They are all. Who, in his own strength, shall contend with them? The mere attempt to do so requires God.

Christianity concerns itself neither with the branches of the tree to influence their bent, nor with its foliage, nor with its trunk even: but it keeps watch of the sap whence all the rest emanate; and branches, trunk, and foliage profit by its care.

Do right implicitly, without accepting any political system, and the political system becomes the sincere representative of that cause of truth and right which will profit by such action. In this world we must know how to wait, and had far better sow than aspire to reap. Only violence moves with rapidity; but the traces of its passage may as quickly disappear. Useful action is slow. Its toil is long unnoticed, but its effects never fail to make themselves felt afar. If you remove from the realm of circumstance and human seduction the ideas which you know to be indisputably right, and devote yourself to these, your conscience is satisfied. Attach yourself, then, to this certain good; opposing to all else a moral resistance, whereby society may count an activity the less, but never a danger the more.

And let us not lightly brave the possible peril of missing God's thought in the region of the unknown. How sad to have given your heart to something that God has not willed, which he did not will even at the moment of your unreserved surrender! Let us keep the passion of our souls for causes whose triumph is not doubtful; and, with each of us, let the object of ambition be to deserve success, rather than to obtain it.

He who works with any other end than this, may regret his efforts even if he succeed. He, on the contrary, who works independently of all partial, possible, contingent aims, in a general way, — doing each hour the good which comes to hand, expressing only what he feels to be true, supporting only what he believes to be just, such an one seems to take thought but for to-day; but, in reality, he is working for eternity. Schiller says, in a noble verse, "He who does good in his own time, has wrought for the ages." Few things in this world are accomplished after a direct and absolute fashion. More people are hit by ricochet than by direct aim; and a random shot finds its mark. Let truth, justice, and charity pervade the heart, and the atmosphere will be perfumed far and wide.

We take great thought for others, if we but watch over our own rectitude, fortify the soul, and purify it of all venom, all weakness, all irritation, all internal susceptibility, and all fear of man. Under these conditions the good work is in danger of being its own reward; but what matter? Of the seeds that are flung to the winds, are there not many which will germinate far, very far, from the stem that bore them?

Slavery, for example. Christianity has no need to ordain its abolition,—it inspires it; and that is enough for the man who would be governed by the spirit of Christ. It is the imperfect reception of Christianity in the soul which allows slavery to continue; and truth has made no progress unless human bondage has been rendered impossible by its advance. To combat slavery solely from a philanthropic point of view, is too often to lose one's labor, for lust and cupidity mount guard over the system; but to encourage, develop, and stimulate the moral element most antagonistic to human bondage, is to accelerate the chances of emancipation, and to multiply them a hundred-fold.

The fact is, that civilization lives, and has lived, only on Christianity; follows it afar off, and one day, perhaps, will be shaped upon its model: but weakness, poverty, and obscurity cannot hasten that day, save by the sacred hope they cherish, and by repeated acts in conformity with the Christian spirit. Elementary notions of faith have often sufficed to raise man to the highest moral dignity; and what faith does in this respect, faith alone can do. All that appears without, has had its beginning within us; and, virtually, nothing can change in human institutions, if our hearts be not changed.

Another and equal benefit of Christianity is, that it achieves nothing by shocks, nor ever advances but to retire. All that it has dictated or established in this world has been done without violence. The true need of a people or an individual is deeply rooted; and progress is slow in proportion to the inherent force. Progress, however vast, when not provoked by human passion, is never cruel in its advent, nor destructive in its advance. Every thing bends to it: resistance is gradually weakened; and it adapts itself naturally to those great events which have become necessary and opportune. It is only when the will of man is rashly and prematurely interposed, that commotion and ravage begin.

Nature, too, like all else here below, is subjected to the law of death; and has her revolutions, her decadence, her progress. When it becomes necessary for her to pronounce a final sentence, she initiates a process of gradual decay. Under her watchful and provident hand, the traces of ravage disappear; birth arises from death; and, even when she makes ruins, she makes no rubbish.

ON RESIGNATION.

COMPILER'S DEDICATION.

To Count Albert de Resseguier and Prince Agustan Galitzin, with the Grateful Acknowledgments of A. de Falloux.

COMPILER'S PREFACE.

THE reader is already aware that no part of what Madame Swetchine wrote was destined for publicity, but I think the statement should be repeated to those who are about to commence the perusal of this genuine Treatise on Resignation.

Nowhere has that incomparable soul revealed itself more fully than in the majority of the ensuing pages. The finest observation of earthly things here shines side by side with the anticipated peace of heaven; and strokes worthy of La Bruyère abound together with flights worthy of St. Augustine. The faculty of living at once the life of the world and the life of God, and the power of passing without effort from one sphere to the other, was never displayed in a form more affecting and original, more fascinating and more instructive. One may say, in a word, to those who knew Madame Swetchine, that here they will find the whole of her.

Unfortunately this work is but a fragment. None may attempt to finish it in its author's stead. Certain transitions are wanting; some highly spiritual points will seem, it may be, imperfectly elaborated or illustrated. It is therefore important to remember that Madame Swetchine, who gave vent to her thoughts and emotions merely for the sake of satisfying and enlightening her conscience, gave herself no uneasiness about introducing the minds of others gradually to her own point of view.

We read awhile ago, that "writing in pencil is like speaking in a low voice."[1] It will convey a just idea of the strictly private purpose of this work to state, that more than half the unfinished manuscript is written with a pencil.

ALFRED DE FALLOUX.

Chap. 1, No. 74, of the "Thoughts."

ON RESIGNATION.

———◆———

"In voluntate tua, Domine, universa sunt posita, et non est qui possit resistere voluntati tuæ, tu enim fecisti omnia, cœlum et terram et universa quæ cœli ambitu continentur. Dominus universorum tu es."—ESTHER ix. 11.

CHAPTER I.

ON RESIGNATION APART FROM CHRISTIANITY.

RESIGNATION is one of the virtues with which Christianity has endowed the world,—not that the human soul did not contain it from the beginning, along with all good and evil principles; but it is only by the light of revelation that it displays the impress of that character of freedom, love, persuasiveness, and power, which the saints, the sages of Christendom, have shown us it can wear.

Man has always suffered, always seen his wishes crossed, always fought Destiny with forces more or less unequal. Yet, though necessarily vanquished in many cases, in respect of having to yield to some external pressure, man remains, at the bottom of his heart, master of the conditions of his defeat, and, by that law of moral freedom which governs his interior life, he is sure of being able to escape any volition but his own. To yield or to defy, to resist or to submit, to adore or to deny, are so many ways which remain open to him. What decides his choice is simply the idea that he forms of the power that governs him, according as he conceives it intelligent or blind, friendly or hostile, implacable or impassible. An instinctive feeling warns us that mere force has no moral element, and that none but a spiritual law can be authoritative to us; and the will within us follows the modifications which our opinions and beliefs undergo, and reacts at the same time upon the impressions it receives; resisting them even when they are rooted doubly — and how strongly! — in nature and in habit.

The first religious system which presents itself to our thought is that of Greece, so ingenious in its fables, with whose mythology we are familiarized by our earliest studies.

In examining the influence exerted by that system upon the human will, we are first struck by that sombre deity which, hovering in sovereign might above the personified passions who peopled Olympus, revealed itself only by arbitrary and irrevocable judgments. The true god, the Master of the gods, even of him who usurped the name of the supreme god, was Fate, — Fate in its profound blindness, and in all the cynicism of its capricious and tyrannical decrees. Jupiter, who shaped and regulated a world which he had not created, and who realized no scheme that we can grasp, presented himself to man neither as a legislator nor as a judge. He had set in motion the elements extracted from chaos, with a careless hand; and evil, whose nature and origin remained insoluble problems, incurred no animadversions from him. The action of Jove on the events of the world was no more free than his intent in its formation had been a moral one. His very will obeyed the irrevocable decrees emanating from a power whose essence was wrapped in profound mystery. Blind force was everywhere; the authority which God exercises over man by direct and explicit commandments, nowhere.

Under the law of a brilliant Polytheism, which forgot nothing but reverence for the gods, and pity for human nature, we see the most advanced and intellectual people on earth, in whom the yearning for right and justice should have been stimulated afresh by its very development, persisting in a system which banished even wisdom and freedom from the heavens. And when such gods, in perpetual warfare with the conscience of mankind, bowed before that Fate whose blindness drove reason to despair, the desire of man could discover nothing above it, neither law nor light nor help. He beheld himself from that moment helplessly given over to the alternative of an insensate struggle or a bitter and abject despondency. Thus in the pictures which antiquity has left us of man contending with misfortune, we see, with a few illustrious exceptions, only the rigidity of pride, or the intoxication born of sensual pleasure. Ajax or Epicurus, — these are the two extremes, to one of which grief could hardly help but lead, according as man aimed at fortitude or insensibility.

As religious beliefs were weakened among the Greeks, they began to resolve themselves into systems of philosophy. That of the Porch exalted more than any other the might of the will, striving to show it triumphant even in its useless resistance to the decrees of Destiny; a vain pretence, which resulted only in a show of chimerical impassibility and a lying negation of sorrow.

Mahometan fatalism — which, like all Islamism, was a corruption of true principles — perverted resignation. The world, in the eyes of the followers of Mahomet, was not, as to the pagan, governed by a blind divinity. But, while recognizing a free and intelligent First Cause, — a spiritual God, by whom all things were made, — they conceived all events to be so irrevocably determined in his breast, that, on the one hand, God fettered his own movements, and lost even the right to relent; and, on the other, he stripped mankind of every vestige of moral freedom.

From this point of view, God effaces no sentence of his to make room for a new; and the word of Pilate is of constant and universal force, "What I have written, I have written."

A supple instrument in the hands of an ardent and able chief, Islamism seized on the passive instincts of the orient, gave to the principle of blind submission all that activity which was withdrawn from the mind and the heart, and turned that submissiveness in the direction of warlike fanaticism. The belief in a sentence which had fixed beforehand the unknown future, rendering all precautions useless, armed the Mussulmans with an indomitable courage, which was still further stimulated by the doctrine that all who met death, sword in hand, obtained salvation.

This belief, and all the indulgences offered to the sensual nature, were the principal elements in that success of Islamism, which had well nigh been crowned by the material conquest of the world. Everywhere, save where warlike fanaticism had to shield religious fanaticism, Mahometanism bore its proper fruit. It extinguished moral activity in the double sleep of idleness and license; and, beginning with improvidence and ending with indifference, it plunged the soul into a lethargic torpor.

The quietism of India — another and equally distorted form of resignation — takes its rise in a subtle and fundamental error, — in a Pantheism which confounds all substances and confuses all relations. The human soul is there considered, not as a creation of the Most High, but as a part of him, as the spark is a part of the fire whence it issues. We can understand how, upon this hypothesis, man becomes the legitimate end of his own being; and that a state of imbecile satisfaction, of internal and external immobility, would be the one consequence of his absorption into the divine unity.

Since every error, in its transition from the realm of speculation to real life, becomes morally dangerous, the logical result of this Indian dogma of absorption is to restrain action and dispel the notion of duty; attacking human energy in the twofold end, it should pursue, — devotion to others and detachment from self. Instead of walking by the light of vivifying precepts, resignation, with the Hindu, borders upon indolence, and seems to follow the dark and downward proclivity of natural tendencies. It annuls intelligence, and exhausts its strength in vain speculations and imaginings, which have no application save to the useless practice of the most fantastic puerilities. Even in regard to the gymnosophists of India, it would be outrageous to reproduce the trite accusations of falsehood and hypocrisy; but, while rejecting these, at the bidding of good sense and experience, the astonishing aberrations of these men do yet prove how poor a defence against the most senseless conclusions are principles independently just, righteous intentions, and an undeniable power of inertia, when one is outside the truth.

If, then, a blind cause cannot incite to respectful and loving submission; if to deny the fact of suffering is quite a different thing from teaching ourselves to bear it; if it is equally true that submission, under the conditions which make it a virtue, springs neither from a fatalism which stereotypes God and the world; nor from a quietism which volatilizes all the truth it grasps, — are we not forced to conclude that resignation, as we conceive it, depends on revealed truth?

Were God and man not understood as they are, — by the double light of history and doctrine, — the power which disposes of our destiny would always have lacked the moral character of authority, and servile fear would never have yielded its place to filial reverence. The single fact of redemption, in its double aspect of love and power, gives us a deeper insight into justice, fitness, merit, and the real meaning of absolute submission, than all human inductions, all prudent calculations, and all the abstract demonstrations and vague apperceptions of a hollow theosophy.

No vague, impersonal God whatever, who wills to reign unknown beyond the suns, can exercise any authority over man abandoned to himself, and ignorant at once of his greatness and his nothingness. To create within us a steady, tender, patient submission, it is needful that the prayer addressed to God by a distinguished saint — " *Noverim te, noverim me*" — should already have been heard in the depths of our being. It is needful that God, so distorted and misunderstood by ignorance and unbelief, should be actually present to the eyes of man, as the living God who evoked ourselves, and all things else, from naught, and stooped to repair his work after the fall. It is needful that man should go back through the ages, and see unrolled the magnificent panorama of most impressive mercies, and God never forsaking his own, even when he seems to have ·abandoned them. It is needful, above all things, that faith should show us in the heavens the God who has spoken to our souls; the good God, the divine Son of Man, — that slain Emanuel, who came to teach us all things, to live, to die, to remain with us.

In default of this divine succor, we may doubtless make our courage a point of honor, and present a calm front to the blows of Fate; but Christian resignation is not confined to apparent fortitude, an unaltered countenance, and isolated acts: it should penetrate all the emotions before they are externally betrayed. This resignation is rather the free expression of a regenerated and victorious will, than an effort of virtue: it is far more a situation of the soul, than the adherence to a course of action considered and adopted on the spur of the moment. It cannot be too often repeated that the permanence of such effects presupposes, as an essential element, a living, enlightened, active faith, — such a faith as

Christianity alone can produce, because it alone, by its admirable distribution of light and shade, shows itself armed equally with justice and with mercy, and marvellously watchful of all that passes on the earth. It belongs to the wisdom which preceded and prepared all things, to draw us to itself while leaving our desires all free; and, if our God did not bear the name of Providence, our hearts could never have conceived of true and lasting resignation.

•

No system of religion has proclaimed more loudly than Christianity the freedom of man. Implied even in that word of the Almighty, "Let us make man in our image,"— it is equally attested by the oldest human fact to which we can recur, — original sin, which is, alas! only a vast and criminal exercise of our freedom.

If man had not a distinct personality, — an individual existence, — the mind to know and the faculty to choose, — if he had not a sphere of action, and a safe asylum in his own conscience, where would be his resemblance to God?

If man were not free, how could he be guilty? how could he have crossed the designs of God and consummated his own misfortune? Without liberty, there is no responsibility: without responsibility, no act would bear a moral impress; and consequently justice in the administration of reward and punishment would be impossible.

The very fact that liberty is the characteristic of his nature distinguishes man from the rest of creation, and invests him with a special, personal life, which renders him, under grace, the master and artist of his own destiny. It is by his free will that man, placed midway between good and evil, can become guilty or meritorious. It is because the will of man can protest, and resist even while yielding to the law which internally it rejects, that his adherence has a meaning and his consent a value, — and that his choice, whatever it be, has weight in the balance.

But this freedom, which in God is absolute, has merely been munificently conceded to man. The primal attribute of his kingship over the world can be but a primal servitude so far as he, from whom he holds it, is concerned. God has placed man at the summit of creation, that he might bring its rays to a focus, and that his worship might thence acquire more unity and value. He created man free, so as to elevate the character of his dependence, and make it a merit in him to confess it. However great man may be, he has received all; and each one of his privileges creates a perpetual obligation.

To the sense of this freedom, which is common to all men, the Christian adds the knowledge of its uses. His eye measures the chasm opened by the fall. He sees the utter impossibility of filling it without grace.

These two terms, man created free and man fallen, form the original groundwork of one and the same story: their revelation shows us all the mind of God and all our own weakness; and from them spring two virtues, which belong peculiarly to the Christian, — humility, whereof the ancient world never heard; and submission, never to be recognized under the disguises of error.

Since pride caused the fall of man, ought not humility to reinstate him? There exists a correlation, secret and strong, between that freedom which compromised all our rights, and that resignation, which, trusting to the means of reparation, restores man to the rank whence he should never have fallen. All Christian morality is the logical expression of the state in which freedom and the fall have placed mankind. This ethical system is a vast network, which embraces the whole of human nature. All its parts are identical, despite diverse proportions: they bear the same impress, down even to those remote deductions, in which we can hardly recognize the substance of the precept, under the ethereal and sublimated form of the decree.

Among these deductions, nevertheless, there are some which issue more immediately from the womb of the Christian doctrine, and are, as it were, its first-born; and humility and resignation claim these honors of primogeniture. These two virtues, in short, not only place in a strong light the most salient characteristics of Christian morality, but they initiate us into its deepest and most secret essence; and are also the effective methods whereby its highest and most explicit teachings receive their full realization. Thus, while humility became man's highest virtue, as pride had been the principle of his fall, resignation voluntarily bound itself to expiate the sins of freedom.

Redemption, the work of adorable and infinite pity, — all whose power is concentrated in the self-abasement of obedience, — shows us, next in order to the three divine virtues, humility and resignation. Humiliation and suffering, — this is the royal way in which our Lord precedes us. Humiliation and suffering constitute, under grace, all the joy of innocence, and all the confidence of sinful man. From them those lowly flowers which grow at the foot of the cross derive all their sweetness.

Born in the first dawning of light upon the world, and resting on the truths which Scripture and tradition have transmitted to us, resignation, as the thought of the Christian conceives it, has nothing in common with the paths trodden by the wisdom of paganism. How could Christianity fail to pronounce Stoicism false and self-contradictory in its true, rational, inmost meaning? How could it fail to find the denial of sorrow specially absurd, in a system which gives us no advantage over grief, because it offsets no hope against it.

Christianity, the work of Him who made nature, does not thus contravene nature's laws, not even by the introduction of a supernatural element. Christianity does not claim to suppress grief, but it purifies and consoles by sanctifying it; justifies it in our eyes by showing us its profound relations with our actual needs; and softens it, as nothing else can, by allowing glimpses of the bliss of which it may one day make us worthy. Truth, alas! can never disavow sorrow, — she who came to sound its depths and show its purpose, and who also knows so well the dignity to which it lifts the soul of man, — and the fruit it should bear therein. In lieu of childishly denying its existence, she strips it of all that could mislead or corrupt, and transforms it by the secret of a divine alchemy. To man, working in God's name, belongs transformation, but not creation or annihilation.

In that system, which recognizes a fatal linking of all effects to their causes, the Christian sees a guilty blow aimed at the power and freedom of the Supreme Being. The shapeless notion of a Creator who is yet absent from his work, of an incomprehensible decree, promulgated once for all, and entailing endless and inflexible consequences, — is fit to paralyze man with terror, and strip him not merely of hope, but of faith in the celestial pity.

Descending into the realm of action, the doctrine of fatalism makes ravages no less deadly, by depriving human activity of all real stimulus. For why, indeed, should we act, why struggle with sloth, inertia, and levity, if our efforts are vain, and nothing within or without us can be modified; if God expects nothing of us; if it is not true that, free and rational agents as we are, God, by giving us his law in our hearts, has revealed his thought to us, and deigned to take us for his co-laborers; if it is not true, in short, that, upon this vast stage of the present, — which projects its shadow upon eternity, — we have God's work to carry on, our own talent to improve, a reward to have earned at the close of every day?

Hypocritical attempts to liken Christian resignation to Mussulman fatalism will never succeed, do what men will in the way of confounding dispositions marked by the most distinctive symptoms. The Turk takes the eve for the morrow. With him inert submission precedes action in lieu of following it, and weakens, if it does not suppress it. The will, in its imbecile adolescence, would shrink from attaining virility. Outside of truth, the will is a suspected force, and is enchained or imbruted, in default of the power to control it. The Christian is less timid. His resignation, active and intelligent to the end, is but the last term of his very activity, — the final consequent of all the attempts he has made and relinquished. It is only after having displayed all his resources, and brought all his powers into play, that the Christian enters upon the rest of perfect submission; a conqueror, whatever be the issue of the strife, since the victory of conscience is the accomplishment of duty, — the completion of the entire task.

It would be equally unjust to attempt to discover aught of Christian resignation in the false pretences of Indian quietism. Despite all, that tender abandonment to the divine will which Christianity bears within, that propensity to unite itself thereto, that joy in self-denial, the sentiments to which it gives birth have naught in common with the absorption of all personality and the haughty pretence to a blasphemous identity. Christianity perfects human virtue by the action of its divine principle; subjugates matter and resists its usurpations, and yet causes it to participate in the sanctification of the soul. Its reverence for realities guards it against puerile dreams; against the pious chimeras with which the imagination teems; against all illusions, however holy their source may appear, and however innocent their effects. It clothes the most subtile thoughts in sensible symbols, ever forcing us, like new Antæuses, to recruit our strength by touching the substance of Deity.

The perfect rectitude of Christian resignation has been quite as strongly menaced in the very bosom of the Catholic Church. First, by determinism, — a system which derives its name from the succession of determining causes, — an obscure and inconspicuous error, though it dares not go as far in predestination as certain modern sects. . . . The fate of the seventeenth century quietism is much better known. It came clothed in fair colors, under the imposing and persuasive authority of dear and reverend names. But the brightest vesture cannot hide error from the vigilance of Israel's sentinels; and for them to signal the reef is to preserve therefrom all that deserve the name of faithful. . . .

We have seen what Christian resignation is not. Let us now attempt to tell something of what it is.

The definitions of faith are not the only ones over which the Church exercises her sovereign dictation. She is equally authoritative in morals; and doctrine comprises both. The Church, then, is at once orthodoxy in belief and infallible rectitude in moral ideas. The creed, translated and transferred to the domain of action, gives moral precepts their value and meaning; guarding the truths it teaches alike from narrow interpretation and undue extension, and from every deviation and misplacement, whereby the order of their importance might be reversed. God, who excludes nothing because he embraces all, causes all simultaneities to march abreast. He has made space for every thing, — in nature, in the duality of man, and in that spiritual world also, where all virtues, as well as all verities, are reconciled one with another. Religion presents them to us in the light of sisters, who have an equal right to the paternal inheritance, who are destined always to support, and never to injure one another; no one of whom can lawfully enlarge her sphere to the prejudice of the others, the integrity of each having been placed in safe keeping of all.

Thus does Christian resignation pursue her way over the reefs of brute fatalism and Indian quietism, favoring no excess, and defending virtue from all encroachment even, as well as from all irregularity. Fair enough to desire only her own proper beauty; strong enough to confine herself to her own limits; at once lofty and lowly enough to treat directly with God; free, living, strong, generous, calm, serene, and incomparably worthy, Resignation wears all these characters in succession, or presents them mingled in one sublime reflection.

Yes: she is proud and worthy, this Resignation, of the bowed head and bended knee. We may not deprive her of the lofty place which voluntary obedience assures to freedom. That cry of the Archangel Michael, "The Lord rebuke thee," is — to quote an eloquent writer — the noblest wish that one creature may form in favor of another. "The Lord rebuke thee;" and tenderness and power shall accompany the rebuke, and his yoke shall free thee from every other.

Yes: resignation is free; for there is no more sovereign act than that whereby we resign our freedom!

Resignation is living and glorious : living, for there is more life in the death of him who, according to the gospel, dies to himself, than in the majority of those shadowy, ghostlike beings, whom conflict, devotion, and sacrifice have never ennobled ; glorious, for the Christian resigns himself as Abraham obeyed. The revealed word has taught him all things ; and its teaching, either in the form of speech or tradition, encounters him again and quite as intelligibly, in the events which God, never rejecting the aid of our weakness, chooses for the manifestation of his will. The conducting wire, which the faithful holds in his hands, is too brightly illumined for him to be troubled by doubts on questions of duty ; and as he is not required to give an account of the chances of success, but merely of the rectitude of his every step, whenever action is constrained to pause, submission comes in its stead.

Finally, resignation is calm and serene, with that visible serenity, whose flame is within and which constitutes the joy of virtue. Resignation lives on reverence and on trust ; but it has also a keen and loving glance, by virtue of which the adorable stratagems which a pitying God employs to reconcile men to his purposes, are rendered clear to its eyes.

Thus the night of our exile has shades, but it has no darkness. While its action goes on and its issue is undecided, strength and moral activity receive their complete development ; but as soon as the conflict ceases, and an aspect of irrevocability proclaims the divine permission or sanction, the Christian bows to these; and his will, uniting with the Supreme Will, takes its place, to use the magnificent words of Bossuet, among the powers of God.

CHAPTER II.

THE JUSTICE AND PROPRIETY OF RESIGNATION. — ITS DIFFERENT DEGREES.

God has willed that nothing on this earth should be either guilty or meritorious, except the human will. That only assumes responsibility by living for good or evil ends. We may even say, with no lack of precision, that there are but two powers in the world, — God and human volition. Where they are in unison, it is a glorious and blessed thing for this earth. When they are at variance, a state of revolt ensues, with all its accompanying chastisements, constituting the height of misfortune for the creature. But, in either case, God is glorified.

From the moment in which man was made acquainted with the abyss into which the founder of the race has plunged his descendants; from the moment when he felt the fatal germ of evil growing within him, and comprehended that this germ was overtopping his own will, it became his duty to embrace that expiation which had become his sole means of rehabilitation, and the pledge of his reconcilement with God.

The rapidity with which he is borne onward, blinds and deafens the sinner,— and what reasonable man does not feel himself to be such?— but the moment he has recovered his self-possession, punishment becomes, in his eyes, the indefeasible right of offended justice, and begets in him a pious hope.

God has but one method of punishing,— abandonment. He meditates in silence on his severities; when he speaks, it is to offer pardon after chastisement, and his most formidable threats are warnings. God chastises, therefore, only that he may give free course to his mercy; and also, that he may reduce and make ready the hearts on which he will act. "Because they have broken this treaty, I have made them feel my power," saith the Lord; but after this severe and cruel trial, he adds, "I will put my law in their inward parts, and write it in their hearts, and I will be their God and they shall be my people."

Is it not evident that the hearts that are softened and subdued by affliction are destined to receive a yet deeper impress of those sacred characters traced by the divine hand?

Chastisement, under the name of sorrow, comprehends all the countless trials inflicted upon human nature. Suffering is unavoidable. Weakness might have been redeemed by strength, ignorance by wisdom, poverty by riches, but only sorrow could be the ransom of sin. The details of the passion, the agony and death of a God, which form the salient points in the great drama of redemption, show us the nature of the means applicable to the accomplishment of our regeneration.

Yet if suffering had been only a punishment in the hands of God our Saviour, he could not have assumed it in his own person once and for all. He would have kept it in reserve for his judgments; and, preceding us in a shining and serene path, he would have caused us to describe a complete circle of brilliant and useful developments. But the remedy in this case would not have reached the root of the evil: the sting would not have been extracted, the red-hot iron would not have been applied to the wound. Therefore did Christ open the royal way of the cross. He entered it before us, sparing himself in no respect, undergoing in his own person all forms of suffering and ignominy, draining them to their dregs, and yet transmitting them in their full strength to us. Expiation! How dear should it be to us! It is our Master's blood, the living trace of his footsteps in the dust through which we follow him, the pledge of our restoration to the paternal inheritance, our rank lost and regained, the turning-point of our sorrowful history. It is Calvary, without which there would have been no resurrection.

The acceptance of suffering — that is to say, submission to the will of God — partakes so entirely of the nature of that piety to which have been promised the good things of this life as well as those of the life to come, that it harmonizes with all the instincts of a lofty nature. Thus an instinct deeply engraven upon the soul is solidarity. But to rebel against the sorrows of the race is to isolate one's self from the rest of humanity; to refuse to bear one's part of the heavy sentence under which it labors, to separate one's self from one's brethren, to be insensible to the blows which fall on them; to choose not to be smitten when they are so, in short to lose the power even of saying with the poet, "*Humani nihil a me alienum puto;*" for we have but a lip-sympathy with the lot which we will not share.

This multiplied echo of all hearts that have ever beat in the heart that is beating still; this burning conviction that each one of us might have committed the crimes committed by all; this *solidarity* which causes the heart to leap unceasingly in sympathy, in exultation, in wrath or in pity; this sentiment, so strong when it is merely natural, receives from Christianity a loftier life and a very different aim.

What! when Abraham obeys, when Job suffers himself to be despoiled, when David bathes his sin in his tears, and the new Isaac consummates his sacrifice upon Calvary, shall we sinners revolt against obedience, poverty, tears, or death? The mother of

Christ survived her divine Son, and shall we not endure to have Christ pierce us with the same sword of sorrow? Ah! were such our disposition, what a threatening contradiction would it not receive from the innumerable throng of martyrs and saints, whose lives were but a paraphrase of that sublime word of Saint Theresa, "To suffer and to die"!

If events are fortuitous, it is plain that they entail no obligation upon us; and it becomes allowable for us to obey the humor of the moment and yield to those transports of childish rage which endow brute matter with sensibility, and return blow for blow upon an offending object or turn away from it in fickle caprice.

If God does not reign, it is quite evident that man becomes the master of all his acts, personifying law in himself, and rejecting all that interferes with his own good pleasure, as beyond the pale thereof. Therefore, to repulse what incommodes himself; to deny or calumniate what surpasses; to avert what wounds, opposes, or afflicts; to crush what is inferior, — all these things we may much the more reasonably expect that man will do, as man is more consistent with himself. But if, on the other hand, the heart, while yet wrapped in its thick veil of flesh, begins to catch glimpses, under the gross exterior of things, of the mind which created them; if it perceives the ruling Power which preserves only because it rules them; if, especially, the evil days whereof man's earthly pilgrimage is composed begin to seem like the prelude to an unending life, — what consequences ensue, what teachings flow from these primary truths! Then do things begin to share the importance, and, so to speak, the intelligence of persons; for they cease to be in our eyes aught save what the eternal Wisdom willed them to be in the order of our salvation. While, if this Wisdom be once eliminated from the government of the world, it is men that are assimilated to things, becoming like these the puppets of blind combinations, whose original impulse is lost in deep, thick darkness.

Revelation alone teaches us to know God and ourselves. Revelation alone discovers the direction of the destinies of humanity in general, and our own in particular; a double movement, magnificently symbolized by the annual and diurnal revolutions of the earth.

After following the finger of God in history, and in the sensible prodigies of each one of our lives; after receiving the sublime promise that not a hair of our heads shall fall without his notice, — what more do we need? Has not God at once calmed all our fears, and irrevocably changed the objects of our regard and aversion? Does not an infallible word like this make us feel that we are watched, guarded, protected by the great sleepless eye of our Father?

Within the horizon illuminated by its brightness, what perplexity is hopeless, what sadness too poignant, what restraint annoying, what sorrow greater than we can bear? Does not God himself take measures to secure our endurance, by giving us the certainty of escaping annihilation, the hope of avoiding condemnation, and I know not what delicious and undeserved presentiment of heaven, as the reward of our languid efforts, and the sufferings we have so justly incurred?

In respect of that eternity which we are to win, nothing is evil save what diverts us from our supreme end; nothing good save what conducts us to it, were it even anxiety or affliction. When the immortality offered to man impresses itself vividly upon his convictions, all the conditions of his earthly existence are changed; and the events it brings forth, cease to be in any sense important, I had almost said real, save in their relation to that end.

Thus, then, man may resist, protest, deny his inmost convictions; but, if demons have not suggested to him a hideous blasphemy, if he believe, he must submit; if he yield, he must fall prostrate. There is no medium. To choose his objects of submission; to check or to suspend it, — is but a kind of neutrality between rebellion and assent, a kind of compromise between the fear which checks complaint, and that other weakness which cannot choose but endure; a mere external attitude, which keeps the soul on sufficiently good terms with what it reveres, but none the less leaves the will diseased, smitten with that moral impoverishment which, under the name of lukewarmness, God has so severely condemned.

Yet let us not exaggerate, nor even here anticipate the progress of that grace which in its invisible and ascendant march reveals to us new horizons in succession, and enables us to accomplish with ease the most difficult undertakings. Let us not forget that, in the celestial kingdom, there is more than one inhabited region, and more than one resting-place on the holy mountain; and that, though the landmarks from base to summit have been immutably placed by the very hands of God, he does not require the entire route of all his children. Virtue has its degrees; and, as far as man is concerned, its hierarchy also.

An artificial human morality betrays its origin as much by its exaggerations as by its hiatuses. Arbitrary in its demands, it either exalts or neglects the precept, and almost always extemporizes it; now imposing heroism by an imperious formula, and again corrupting the moral law by an impure alloy. The Catholic religion, on the contrary, taught by its divine Founder to distinguish the precept which is universally binding, from the advice which may be followed at option, puts its children on their guard not only against laxity, but against those extravagances in the theory of right which have often been but a noble and attractive aspect of its decay. Resignation, at its point of departure, is far distant from that lofty height which it may attain. Like the other Christian virtues, it resembles a pyramid, whose broad base is the precept, but which rises and contracts by degrees into a mere point; an image of the perfection and consummation of counsel.

The first degree of submission is reverent acquiescence in the divine will. Afterwards, this sentiment is transformed into a pious and sincere acceptance, whereof trust is the prime motor. The soul now yields more than she reasons; seeing in Him who imposes the trial, less the Creator who has a right to exact the whole, than the adorable Saviour who preaches submission by his own obedience. In her eyes, God has ceased to be any thing but the Wisdom who can neither deceive nor be deceived, and yet that loving Wisdom who sees in man the masterpiece of his own power, and has prepared all things so as to insure his salvation. . . .

Soon we see the struggle, which is not incompatible with this condition, fail, and fade away in slighter and slighter oscillations, in a twilight impenetrable, yet a thousand times penetrated. Once started in the way of self-abnegation, trust, from respectful, becomes filial; and the acquiescence in all that God sends, passes, as it were, into a holy habit.

The will, which acts only as far as it sees, — and which sees clearer and farther in proportion to its activity, — cannot be enlightened without having its strength doubled by the enlargement of its comprehension. It surmounts all obstacles, and frees itself from all shackles successively and finally: as the last term of its efforts, it is delivered from itself. Lightened of its load, more intelligent because more independent, fed by so many mercies, feeling that its revolt has been weak from the first, conquered even then, and now expiring, it reaches that blessed point where we cease to see aught save what God wills, or to desire aught that he has not desired. Then only it is, after having thus overcome the world within himself, that the Christian — Christ's noble free man — lays intact at the feet of his Master the power which he has regained, and presents, in the inextricable interweaving of grace and free-will, the truest assimilation of human nature to God.

Thus, in these different and variously illumined elevations, we have successively the inclination of reverential faith, the submission of pious faith, and the unity of victorious faith, — but always faith; since faith is made the soul of resignation for the precise purpose of rendering it, in its principle and effects, a supernatural virtuè, which, perchance, comprehends all others.

God has done so much to diminish the number of the guilty! He desires, smiles upon, and aids our progress, yet does not need it. But when once, through the blessing of a fulfilled precept, we have discerned somewhat of the fair order of God's purposes; when our first initiation has acquainted us with the nature of his views, — how can we stop at the letter of the law, how fail to respond to those most affecting solicitations of his love, which plead for our full surrender? When we have taken the step of quitting the ways of nature, — ways which, after all, 'tis often easy and sweet to follow; when we have schooled ourselves to silence, and conquered ourselves at a thousand appreciable points, — is it worth while to pause in the region of a doubtful and debatable obedience, and, after having renounced the world and its fascinations, to miss, when thus despoiled, even the true liberty of the children of God?

A constellation of virtues watches over this resignation; and shall not the Christian, who reads each day, "The just shall live by faith," add, if his heart suffers, by faith and by resignation?

Faith renders resignation reasonable.

Hope renders it easy; charming our griefs by giving us a foretaste of actual joys, and lightening all burdens by the power of that attraction which urges us on towards the unseen good.

Charity, the all-powerful, communicates its spirit to resignation.

The love of God, after turning us aside from the long-cherished love of ourselves, levels the hills, that naught may interrupt our view of the divine horizon;

and fills the valleys, that our march may not be hindered.

Patience touches resignation so closely that they seem almost identical. It is in patience that we possess our souls, — patience, a delicious fruit when gathered ripe, whose root only is bitter, as an ancient writer says.

Humility is the true torch which illumines our sorrows. Insolvents that we are, what can we suffer that we have not deserved, if not in detail, at least on the whole? Humility, gentle and tender, plucks out the dart and heals the wound, cicatrized by resignation.

Sacrifice! We must not forget that the Christian altar is a tomb, and that the adorable Victim invites us to immolate ourselves along with him upon the bones of confessors and martyrs. The spirit of sacrifice is meet for all; and, while heroic deeds are demanded of some, there remains for the rest an obscure and perpetual immolation.

Passing fancies, incomplete sacrifices, the many things which compromise the free and full ideal, cannot, of themselves, bear blessed fruit or effectual consolation. When one has gone so far as to wish to turn away from self, he must turn to God irrevocably and entirely. He must become that inhabitant of the holy city, who "bears," as St. Augustine says, "in the depths of his heart, a perpetual fiat and amen;" who wants all the pains he endures, and none of the consolations which are denied him. Ask him what he desires, and he will tell you, — exactly what he has. God's will, in the present moment, is the daily bread which transcends all substance.

CHAPTER III.

ON THE ADVANTAGES OF SUBMISSION.

THAT submission which God seems to require for his own sake, he, in reality, desires for ours. It is wholly for our interest, and answers our most pressing need.

If our nature were not so deeply degraded, if sin did not dim our vision by incessantly deepening the shadows around us, internal and external motives for resignation would still arise from the very nature of things. How could weakness help confiding in strength, darkness in light, deep ignorance in the wisdom from which nothing is hid?

And that which the holy Scriptures most clearly reveal to us, is the goodness of God and the love he bears to man. He created man to know, serve, and love him, and thereby to merit a blessed eternity. He makes him responsible only that he may crown him. Can we suspect that Providence, after tracing so sublime a programme for his creatures, demands aught from them but obedience, as the means of realizing it? Liberty, in a created being, is intimately correlated with obedience. Without a restraining law, liberty would be a fatal gift,—a kind of shirt of Nessus. All equilibrium would be destroyed.

Of all the traits which go to make up the grand and divine figure of Christ, none is more marked than obedience. Not merely his acts, of which the last and sublimest conducted him to death,—and death on the cross!—but all his words express simply the immolation of his will. "I came down from heaven," says he, "not to do mine own will, but the will of Him that sent me." Thus it was not enough for Christ, that, by the consubstantiality of his divine nature, his will was identical with that of the Father. The Son of God,—God himself,—he came down to earth, both to teach us how to love God's will better, and to introduce us to all the blessings of submission.

Faith, which shows us our own destiny, reveals at the same time the whole economy of the divine plans; shows that each and every one of us is as much the object of providential solicitude, as if he were its single centre; and declares, not merely that God wills our salvation, but that, relatively to us, it is the only thing he wills. On the one hand, he imposes on man the obligation of striving to secure his own happiness. On the other, he pledges himself to render infallible, in some sort, the means of success.

The poor human creature, whose life is but a day, whose soul may be lost or required of him at any moment, should find in life, under a God who is faithful to his promises, only a divine preparation, most meet to develop, strengthen, correct, and purify the spiritual germ, and raise it to the level of that destiny which the Eternal is preparing for him. Man fails in his vocation, but God cannot fail in his promises. All the heedlessness and ingratitude of his creatures cannot alter the fact, that, at each moment of their earthly course, all the means of perfection are given or offered them. These means may be disguised; but, in whatever shape they appear, they never lose their essence, nor, if man so wills, their mighty virtue.

Hence it follows, that all the situations in which God places us, all the dangers even to which we are exposed, if they be not the punishment of the rash provocations we have offered, may be turned to our advantage; and that what *is*, for the very reason that it is, conduces to our highest interests.

It cannot be otherwise, from the moment that you acknowledge a sovereign Ruler in heaven, and a dependent creature on the earth. The Creator, who is truth and power itself, cannot be mistaken about the end which the poor creature, so benevolently summoned into existence, ought to attain, any more than in the nature of the aid which is indispensable to him. God, as Christianity represents him, — the only true Father of his children, — is working for their happiness every instant of that time which he has summoned from his own eternity. Man, in the words of St. Paul, is at once the field that he cultivates and the edifice that he builds. Nature, man, the very elements; the earth ploughed, sown, and weeded by the divine Laborer, — all these are God's means. All irregularities contribute to the beauty of the harvest, and the north wind and snows of winter are as needful as the sun to cause the precious seed to fructify. Hence, every vicissitude in its season.

On the other hand, the Saviour says to us, "There shall in no wise enter into it any thing that defileth;" "Put off the old man;" "Verily I say unto you, except a man be born again, he shall not see the kingdom of God." What, then, do we find? Two terms, divided by an abyss, — but an abyss which the selfsame word assures us can be bridged by infinite pity and human desire: firstly, a God who so loved men that he came to live, suffer, and die among them; secondly, a nature weak and imperfect, but endowed with moral faculties, which render it susceptible of progress, and able to respond to the sublimity of its vocation.

Hence, joy and sorrow, as understood by the world, are capable of a deeper and truer interpretation, which acquaints us with the secret of the Creator's merciful designs in reference to his creatures.

For the very reason that the Master is benevolent and mighty, and the creature capable of education, this world assumes the aspect of a vast school, where all within and without us is destined to become conducive to our advancement. We need not merely to be taught, but to be healed, — human nature being "that great invalid," so called by the pious Augustine, who understood it so well. And the great invalid appeals to the great Physician. Redemption is the pledge of cure. Resignation is naught but the will to seize all offered remedies.

Divine wisdom, embracing all of man in the law it gives him, embraces no less the totality of his destiny. God makes no virtue obligatory upon man, which does not greatly subserve his temporal welfare. But he considers this transitory being only in his relations with immortality; and if he arms him as a warrior for time, it is only to enable him to conquer that kingdom of heaven that "suffereth violence."

Earthly happiness — mixed, brief, uncertain, always so near annihilation — could not have been the final end which Providence proposed in our creation. His greatness disavows so low an aim. His love reserves for man, greater liberality and magnificence. But taking us so low, and raising our hopes to so high a pitch, what a variety and abundance of care, help, and invention, has he not found needful, to help us to mount the ladder of restoration! How can we comprehend both the ostensible and secret resources that were requisite to move our so stupid and rebellious human nature, — to restore, raise, attract, instruct, guide without compulsion, bend and enlighten it, and, as it were, prevent its falls without its knowledge? "What have I not done for thee, O my people!" says Christ to each one of us. "What could I have done that I have not done?" The Father of the great human family, he yearns over his children, dispensing to them the bread of Christian knowledge, and pouring for them, though with a trembling hand, the wine of tribulation.

Human events are but a succession of remedies, appropriate to our variously diseased state, — a succession of lessons applicable to the different forms of our ignorance; and the world is the theatre of that divine experiment, where the Restorer shows himself as great as the Creator, and more merciful than he. All things work together for good to them that love God.

The greatest of earthly ills are entirely out of proportion with that eternal weight of glory which, if we will, is one day to reward us. Who of us would not a thousand times rather have salvation than the world, even though he be not entirely weaned from the latter?

Therefore, let us fairly and sincerely review in memory those human pangs and griefs which have isolated or transfixed our hearts, and acknowledge that the cruellest severities in the order of nature have been salutary; that we owe much of what we are to what we have missed; and that in our sharpest sorrows the help was found which snatched us from the abyss. God's children receive blessings only from his liberal hands, — blessings unrecognized in the language of men, but which our guardian angels know how to call by their true names. "The chastisements of the Almighty are blessings in disguise."

Observe, first of all, that this Will, before which we are required to bow, asks of us nothing impossible, unreasonable, or humiliating. In no case does Christian perfection demand acquiescence in a culpable or dangerous position, or indifference to God's sentence of disgrace, or to the deprivation of his sacraments, and of the uncounted wealth with which he has dowered his church. Resignation is applicable only to things that pass away. Neither has it ever denied the rights of human sensibility; nor can it be too often repeated, that it is not so much excess of grief that resignation resists, as its revolt. God brings such beautiful results out of grief, when it is simple and deep, that it always finds grace; and there is indulgence for our tears, even when weakness has made them flow.

But when, irritated by pain and given over to a

prideful bitterness, we take a haughty attitude before the Most High, and seem to require of him an account of our trials, and to treat with him on equal terms, do we do well to exult in the plenitude of our reason, and to mark the distance between our nothingness and the might and wisdom of the Infinite?

Ah! if, rather, we are docile to the voices of humility and justice, and assume before God that attitude of sinners which belongs to us, what truths will be revealed to us by our sufferings, what mysteries will be explained! Suffering, that divine messenger,—"*Der gottliche Bote, das Elend,*"—will then appear to us the messenger of reconciliation.

The sacred Scripture calls him most miserable to whom it has not been given to dread the supreme sentence. In short, while this fear lives in us, how can the justice of our own hearts help saying that God's justice demands satisfaction; and, if the conditions of this satisfaction were left to our own sole choice, how could we feel confident of their fitness or efficiency? If we dread the position of insolvent debtors, resignation offers us the means of acquittal; and these means are precisely that grief and bitterness and loathing which we are invariably obliged to undergo.

The selection of our expiatory and purifying sufferings is made by a master hand,—the selfsame hand that traces the way wherein we must walk. Our task is greatly lightened by this fact; and we feel assured that our trials, being divinely shaped upon our needs, adapted to our stature and proportioned to our strength, are calculated to produce all the intended effects. Are we then so sure of what we need? Our constantly disappointed conjectures, our views daily convicted of error, ought, of themselves, to wean us from our own judgment. For who has ever been able to arrange the slightest detail of his life to his own satisfaction; to calculate accurately within the narrowest circle of interests the effects of a given resolution, enumerate its chances, or prevent the inconveniences it may entail; in short, to provide against the uncertainties of any future?

Moreover, the very realization of our wishes must often have sufficed to deprive our prudence of the courage to form new; for, if we have all suffered from cheated hopes, have we not also to deplore the fulfilment of some few? Antiquity illustrated, under a multitude of forms, the ignorant rashness of our passionate desires; and the fable of Semele underlies the experience of every age. It is against the success of our own plans that the Christian's God defends us, — he who refuses to hear, — just as he wounds, — to heal. "We ask in folly, but we are answered in wisdom." God has from all eternity replied to these cries of ours — blinder than they are helpless — by the words, "Your thoughts are not as my thoughts, neither are my ways your ways." It is precisely because his ear is attentive to our insatiable need of faithfulness, that he so often rejects the vain chimeras in which that need finds expression. "All is done for the elect," but done by means of the sorrows they pass through and dwell among; and I ask, in the words of Bildad, that hypocritical friend of Job, — who was not worthy of the truth upon his lips, — "Can the rush grow up without mire? Can the flag grow without water?"

You complain of terrible and unexpected blows; but how can one blast the rock or temper the iron, save by fire and anvil? And you who groan over the crushing continuity of your woes, is it not because you have not yet divined their last secret? "Trouble never comes alone," according to a popular proverb. Trouble, like that demon of the Scriptures, is named Legion. "These things," says the book of Job, "doth God twice and thrice upon the children of men." This, in order that virtue, like knowledge, may be acquired only by a sequence of experiences, and by lessons, the first condition of whose utility is their repetition.

If the winds of prosperity did not blow some portion of the time, how could we feel sure that our virtue was not a thing of chance, and that our hearts were really purified of the leaven that puffeth up, and all the pride of life? So, if our trials and temptations came only at long intervals, and yielded too readily to consolation, where would be the novitiate of patience, and the employment of our energies? How could the divine germ, whose very irregularities are specially conducive to its growth, strike those deep roots which are to bear its branches upward to eternal life? It is by redoubled blows that our rebellious nature is fashioned, and in the persistence of God his will is to be read. It is not merely a question of tempering the iron, but of transforming it into steel; and we know that what demands the last perfection of the workman's skill is that final polish so difficult to obtain.

"Et fons de domo Domini egredietur et irrigabit torrentem spinarum." Who knows whether the living waters of that fountain would have flowed as clearly and swiftly over any other bed?[1] . . .

Is it not our Lord himself who has taught us to say, "Thy will be done"? It is the tenderest and fondest word that love ever pronounced, whereby we salute and bless in advance a will as yet unknown. And that kingdom of God, whose coming we each day invoke, what is it but his will regnant within us, — sovereign by virtue of our resignation? Is it not

---

[1] A friend furnishes the following note: —
Joel iii. 18. In the English version, "A fountain shall come forth of the house of the Lord, and shall water the valley of Shittim." The word Shittim, שִׁטִּים, is the plural of Shittah, שִׁטָּה, the Hebrew name of the *acacia*, or *spina Ægyptiaca*. Hence, *Nahal Hashshittim*, נַחַל הַשִּׁטִּים, *The Valley of Acacias;* in the Latin version, *torrentem spinarum.* — TR.

also that peace that the Saviour promised to his disciples, — "*La sua volonte è nostra pace*"?

For who ever yet resisted God and lived in peace? Let us, therefore, say with the apostle, "We are troubled on every side, yet not distressed. We are perplexed, but not in despair; persecuted, but not forsaken; cast down, but not destroyed."

Resignation is a generous profession of our faith in the kindness of God's purposes towards us. The more searchingly we are tested, the greater should be our courage, and the more plainly we should perceive the thought of Providence. Against chance, we can have neither strength nor courage. But the moment we begin to suspect a divine intention, we are, I think, almost ready to accord wisdom, pity, and foresight to that word of the enigma which is still undeciphered. The less modifiable events appear to be, the less possible it is for us to assign human causes for them; and the greater the opportunity for the exercise of our faith, because God's share in them is more clearly revealed. The more impenetrable his will is, the more goodness and mercy it hides. The pruning of his adorable hand is ever profitable to the tree. Let us be watchful for the slightest summons to action; and, in those hard times when action is impossible, let us imitate the valor of those troops who, by the order of their chiefs, stand motionless, like a living wall, arms in their hands, and exposed to the full fire of the enemy, and are adjudged none the less worthy of the victor's crown when victory is won.

CHAPTER IV.

ON RESIGNATION TO SO-CALLED IRREPARABLE ILLS.

The hardest test of resignation is found, no doubt, in sorrows that have no cure. Irrevocability adds one degree to grief. It puts the finishing touch.

The most trifling evil grows and spreads, if judged utterly irremediable. It is of the essence of irreparable misfortune to check the development of the powers and paralyze all action. It renders our struggles insensate; yet immobility, in the presence of suffering, is, from a human point of view, one of the severest of tortures; no genuine consolation being possible for cureless ills. The natural life offers no hope of solace for what will endure while life endures.

Faith alone can change and widen our horizon. Faith alone enables us to catch glimpses of that region where what was ended on the earth is renewed and recommenced, — where he who dropped down wounded, arises healed; so that already from that upper sphere, where solemn and complete restitution is accomplished, reflections fall upon us that soothe our heavy hearts.

A famous writer has said that the Christian, like Alexander, reserves nothing to himself but hope; a magnificent share, for which the boundaries of the universe are too narrow.

Among all the events which bear the terrible character of irremediability, the death of those we love doubtless stands foremost. To see a part of our being snatched away; to survive, through grief, the affections which constituted our glory, our strength, our joy, or our security, and perhaps all of these, — this is to feel ourselves broken, impoverished, transfixed. These legitimate regrets are more than permitted: it is our dignity to cherish them; and Christianity merely arms us against their excess. Only here as elsewhere, by changing our point of view, Christianity gives us a deep insight into the nature of our affections, in order to sanctify and purify them from all that might irritate or envenom.

Christianity is always ready to admit to us the justice, poignancy, and severity of our griefs; always ready to acknowledge that a void in the joys we have tasted may become an abyss, that the vanishing of a single being may make the world a desert, and that the cruel bereavement may lade every moment with a heavy and heart-rending weight. But, after all these concessions, it demands of us, whether, on the other hand, it is quite right for an immortal creature to pause at any one gloomy point in space, and allow its darkness to overspread his whole career; whether that irrevocability of death, undeniable on this side the grave, preserves its character beyond it; whether faith has ever named eternal separation; whether the friends we mourn, are lost, or only absent; whether, in short, since we have the hope of regaining them one day, we ought not to force ourselves to restrain our impatience, and hasten by prayer our common deliverance.

And can we forget our own death, — that death which has been called the middle of a long life, and which at all events, how long soever our days may be, only strikes, at the outset, an unending existence? When we reflect what man's life under present conditions would be if there were no death, we are abundantly reconciled to the fact. At once a punishment, and a most expressive token of the fall of man and the vengeance of God, it none the less resembles that lance of the poet's fancy which healed the very wounds it made.

Death lavishes useful lessons along the route we have to travel, guiding our steps also, illuminating the horizon before us with most celestial brightness, and causing to pale those unsteady fires and deceitful glimmers which arise out of the sinful earth to seduce and lead us astray. Death teaches us at once the vanity of all that with which it sports, and the grandeur of all that which it respects. The thought thereof is our enlightened judge and infallible counsellor; and if we were not continually mistaking the twilight for the day, we should see how serviceable are Death's living lessons to the one brief morning which makes up our life.

Old age, also, is an irreparable evil. Nothing can make us re-live our years; but, like all obscure situations, it brings with it strong consolations, and a secret charm known only to those who experience its enjoyment. If the life of the old man has been virtuous, the long look he bends upon the past is full of sweetness. He contemplates all its elements, all its pledges of a happy and eternal future. Pausing on the height whence the land looks broadest and richest, he follows the course of the streams he has been able to subdue; he recognizes his favorite places of shade and shelter, the fields tilled in the sweat of his brow, the oaks which have grown from the acorns he planted. The selfsame sun still illumines with his oblique and always friendly rays the long way he has come, and the mysterious paths whereby a good Providence has led him to himself.

If, on the contrary, the old man's days have been evil in the twofold respect of the sins and sorrows they have brought with them, and if, nevertheless, he has not obstinately closed his heart, he assists at the living verification of the divine precepts, at the noble spectacle of God justified in all his ways, and the law avenged at all points by the consequences of his transgressions. He distinguishes clearly amid the sufferings he has undergone, those which God and nature did not prepare for him, and discerns that long chain of invitations by which he has been summoned, and of which, perhaps, it has sufficed that one only has not been refused.

Ah! it enters not into the plan of Providence to disinherit any of his creatures. If latent forces and veiled graces did not lurk beneath the ashes of age, life would never be prolonged so far. God has provided for the duration of all his insensible creatures and for the consolation of all who are not so. In this world, where trial is everywhere and final chastisement nowhere, the real equality between the different conditions of life is greater than would be supposed from the apparent diversity. Situations are to be judged, not from without, but from within. "Taste and see," saith the Psalmist. Taste that you may see. Compensation never fails.

One of the privileges of old age is the possession of truth *par excellence*, — truth stripped of all prestige by the presentation of the naked reality. And shall we make no account of the dangers vanquished, the more immediate divine consolations, the thousand palliatives ingeniously arranged by the Master for his degraded servant? Shall we make no account of the slackened but surer pace, the dignity, the calm, which make old age what God intended it should be, — a sublime halt between a conquered world and eternity?

And see how these bodily infirmities, the slightest one of which would spoil the most marvellously prosperous lot, react upon the heart that accepts them! They do indeed place us in a position of physical inferiority, impose upon us constraint and dependence, break down and overthrow what is haughty within us; but they need not, unless we will, encroach upon the charities of life, or its pious, humble, secret consolations. So far from this, it would seem as if these infirmities enabled us to live in the very atmosphere of the gospel beatitudes. If they make us timid before the eyes of men, they place us more directly under those of God. We are then, by nature, what St. Francis d'Assisi became by circumstances and by virtue, "*poverelli di Christo*," poor, and the real poor; since poverty being the lack of what is needful, we have become, so to speak, its impersonation.

One must needs have tried corporeal infirmity, parted with his keenest repugnance, and afterwards become reconciled thereto, if he would know on what peaceful terms one may live with humiliation, habitual suffering, and constant inconvenience. The progress that is made by the long-continued exercise of submission in a single matter, surpasses all anticipation, and can only be equalled by the tender reverence we are capable of conceiving for an infirmity whose irksomeness has been conquered by patience and by love.

Our sense of honor would be alike wounded, whether we were actually found in conditions which the laws of the world pronounce disgraceful, or whether appearances only were against us. Honor, that steep and rocky isle, whose shore is no more to be seen a second time than that of death, — honor decrees that all stains should be indelible, and that every wound should keep its scar. The spirit of this world framed the code of honor, marked it with its own incisive impress, and imparted thereto its own implacability.

The world, it is true, sometimes forgets; but it expunges nothing, and never forgives. It cannot forgive: nor is this strange; for, dispensing no actual good or real recompense, it has no means of self-defence, save inexorable punishment. But precisely because this harsh, capricious, impotent master has nothing better to offer us, we are invited to seek in the free space above us, a refuge from the irrevocable judgments that are pronounced here below. If we rate the world truly, who shall say how much its castigations have had to do with the tardy justice we render? Is it likely that, if a shining approbation had always accompanied us, we should have sought God with as much zeal and as much perseverance as now?

Honor may be compromised, and virtue none the less intact or recovered; and virtue is always ready and able to protect us. Nothing can prevent conscience from offering its testimony, and placing us under the law, either of innocence or repentance.

If there is a misfortune to which the word irreparable may strictly be applied, and which we cannot mention without a shudder, it is final impenitence, — death in sin and enmity to God. This misfortune carries no great sorrow, save to the heart of the observer. When it is personal, the perverted will is itself stupefied, and, as in desperate and mortal diseases, renders the patient ignorant of his malady, and without apprehension of his danger. But what a sight for the beholder is the impious consummation of all the sinner's revolts, — the heavy tombstone sealing up his crimes, — the Saviour denied or defied at the very threshold of eternity! Ah! if Providence has willed that the only misfortune which is without hope should also be without consolation, he has at least spared no precautions to avert from us the execution of that sentence: there is no curious care which his goodness has not taken to reserve its secret to himself, as if in order to secure the greater freedom of his own action.

Unable to cast aside his justice, one would say that it had pleased God to veil it on the one hand,

and elude it on the other. He admits so many signs of repentance with which he shows himself ready to be satisfied. The Church, our holy mother, wills that all amendment should be hopeful. Even in the dying man, who tries the faith of all about him, a word, a look, a regret, an almost imperceptible gleam, suffice to give a little confidence. If his hand have clasped the crucifix, if his lips have pressed it for the first and last time, if he have responded by one feeble sign to the sacramental words, the Supreme Judge is softened, and ready to revoke his sentence.

Even these extreme limits of mercy the Church finds means to pass. She does more than reduce the number of our anxieties and welcome all that can reassure us. When the misfortune is consummated, however desperate and absolute its conditions may be, she raises her voice and imperiously forbids us to individualize our fears, — glad to proclaim that there are no proper names in Hell.

This eminently Christian reserve is extended with yet better reason to those who are still drinking from the poisoned cisterns. All living beings are capable of improvement, and may, by haste, overtake the most advanced. This is the very reason why God lets men live. Not only are we ignorant of what passes between God and the soul of the impenitent sinner who appears before his tribunal, but a dense cloud hides from our eyes our own individual state.

What human being has ever yet known whether he was adjudged worthy of love or of hatred, and how long he was to persevere! It is a mystery which even the angels cannot penetrate, and which will remain till the judgment-day sunk in the depths of the unfathomable Trinity.

No, — and this is the weightiest of those considerations which ought to reconcile us to irreparable misfortunes, — we could not, in our deeply fallen state, dispense with their terrible teaching, or that influence of theirs which tends constantly to our deliverance. If there were no irremediable evils, — evils, that is, that are present in their completeness in the depths of our own being, — nothing could successfully withstand our vicious instincts. Evil, with a fatal fertility, would propagate itself unceasingly; and there would be no influence strong enough to fix our inconstant thoughts and fickle hearts.

Ah, let us not be always forgetting the things that we believe we always remember! Nothing shows us the vanity of life so clearly, as those poignant ills which stifle and rend us, and are momentarily appeased only to reappear and seize their prey. How plainly they say to us that joy is a trivial thing in comparison with the sway that sorrow may usurp! How clearly they show that the balance is disturbed between loss and possession, — between the things that cause us to die daily, and those which give us an illusive sense of life!

All thoughts which God, in his goodness, can desire to suggest to his creatures, seem to be contained in our struggle with the irreparable. It is the divine diapason with which all just and fair estimates are in harmony. Temporary ills may reveal the Almighty, enable us to attain a partial end, determine to some brilliant sacrifice, or incite to virtuous acts; but the cases are rare in which they produce effects that are integral and profound. Slowly the valleys are filled, the mountains levelled, the oceans change their beds, and the configurations of the earth are determined; and slowly, also, is regeneration accomplished in the human soul. It is this very grief of yours, which, freeing you from the bonds of self, will become the soul of your devotion, and render your piety more firm and your course more straight,—which is already bearing you instinctively to the realms of peace and freedom, and has become at once the ballast, the sail, and the rudder of your voyage toward the new heavens and the new earth. This suffering that follows you everywhere, which you no longer resist, knowing too well that it cannot leave you, hearken unto it as to the voice of a friend and guide, for ever calling to you in the depths of your being. Translate the impressions it gives, penetrate its spirit, trust its inspirations, and you will presently know by experience that nothing conduces more powerfully to the formation of the new and inner man, than the clutch of a sad and inexorable reality.

We will not review the whole list of hopeless ills. Who does not know them to be infinite in number and susceptible of a thousand unexpected and terrible combinations? Suffice it to say that a spirit of genuine submission can reach, soften, and subdue them all. The lever only requires for a fulcrum a steadfast and childlike confidence in the divine pity.

Our misfortunes, of whatever nature, may, after all, be summed up in the impression that they leave on us; and it is precisely in the character of this impression that all merit of our own must consist, because this is the only point where it is given us to act. External events furnish us sorrow in the rough, and we must labor to transform it as we would any other raw material. A great physician [1] has said, "The soul makes her own body." We may say with equal truth, The soul makes her own sorrow. She modifies it, causes it to wear her own colors, or rather imprints upon it the character of her own guiding law.

Not to mention exceptional faults and their consequences, the share which our own shortcomings and imperfections have in the bitterness of our more real afflictions is prodigious. Their unendurable element is almost always one which God did not

---

[1] Stahl.

supply; and frequently a pain which is legitimate, and in itself cruelly intense, requires for its mitigation, if not for its exorcisement, only one more personal effort, or act of self-examination, or one more step towards God.

The Lord can bring the greatest good out of the greatest evil. Let us walk in his footsteps, and by the light of his precepts. Let us transmute, by means of a true and deep submission, our griefs into graces, our trials into virtues, our every sacrifice into an offering, till we ourselves cease to be aught but a hearty and free oblation. "Ah," says a voice most dear to the Catholic faith, "if we did but know how to conform our own to the eternal mind, in lieu of being only patients, we might at least be victims!"[1]

CHAPTER V.

ON THE DIFFICULTY OF RESIGNATION TO SORROWS CAUSED BY OUR FELLOW-BEINGS.

FAR more than we are disposed to believe, we feel as we think; and it would be hard to estimate how much we increase the power and intensity of our own troubles by interesting ourselves in them, insisting that we do well to bewail them, feeding them

---

[1] Count de Maistre, on the death of Eugène de Costa.

by the imagination and indulging them through the refinement and susceptibility of our hearts; nor how much, on the other hand, the genuineness of the most sincere impression is impaired by the judgment which shows it to be exaggerated or puerile.

Let us be watchful; for the active hunger of our hearts will find aliment in any thing: we are capable of seeking excitement in what irritates and wounds, as well as in what flatters and fascinates. Since sin has caused us to live in ourselves, through that ardent and guilty personality which substitutes its own false and passionate unity; for the true unity for which we were created, bitterness and irritation influence us as powerfully as the charm of the tenderest sentiments.

Each human instinct has become, since the original fall, a two-edged sword. By its power of antagonism, it perpetually engenders its opposite; and so we constantly see a quenchless thirst for what is sharp and bitter, proceeding out of a great need of happiness, and hatred born of love.

People of lofty intelligence, who look at things from a human point of view, generally make their philosophy to consist in bravely bearing the reverses brought about by circumstance; and their honor, in keenly resenting the pains which come to them through human agency. Whether the pride or the heart suffers thereby, we exalt this excessive sensibility of ours; and while dissimulating our weakness at all other points, we should be almost disposed to exaggerate it in this respect.

This natural estimate is not wholly unjust. Nothing on this earth has received so high a place as man. Nothing can concern us more nearly than our kind, nothing affect us more closely than our neighbor. Nothing can be worth more to a human heart than another heart. Nothing is more imposing than common opinion. In reverses which are merely circumstantial, events seem to follow their own passive course, innocent of the complications they may entail. It seems as if they could not have been other than they are. But, on the other hand, in those griefs which have been brought upon us by individuals, every thing assumes an intentional character. It is an intelligence which rises up against us, a will which takes an attitude of special hostility to ourselves. The interests that cross our own, the difficulties and oppositions that arise, the springs that are touched, — all these things are managed by a hand whose every motion we can follow and calculate. Here, of course, is the illusion; for these men, though masters of their intentions, and never losing their responsibility, are as much the instruments of divine justice as inanimate and unreasoning objects. It is an optical delusion which causes us to believe the contrary, but one which cannot be resolved and dispelled, save by eyes accustomed to the sacred and visible darkness of faith.

The ways are infinite in which we suffer by others' means; and, firstly, by their faults. Some of these I admit are very trying; and yet does not the really keen and often intolerable part of this kind of suffering come from ourselves, and may it not be our own faults which cause us to suffer so much by those of others? We should be more at ease if we were unmoved by the wrongs we suffer, and this is the only element of trouble which puts us at the mercy of the aggressor. If this is so, let us turn our attention to those accomplices in evil who make us enemies to ourselves. We can act efficiently only upon ourselves; and, after all, it is easier and more desirable to reform ourselves than others. Let us redouble our indulgence toward those whose defection is, we feel, likely to engender our aversion. Let us endeavor to temper with compassion the sentence of justice, reflecting that the individuals who have engaged and been vanquished in this sad struggle, inflict upon themselves far more torture then they cause.

And let us not stop here. Those defects that we recognize and note, let us take care that they do not bring forth faults. Let us watch kindly over others, to shield them from themselves, to remove their occasions of falling, to prevent the outbreaks to which they yield and whereby God is so easily offended. But, instead of this, how many times our ill-humor has excited these transgressions! What malicious allusions it has made, what harsh reproaches uttered, taking as a personal affront that which belonged only to the conditions of character!

One of our most common and irrational propensities is to seek for an offensive intention in a general disposition, which exposes to suffering all who come in contact with it; and to desire to enforce the duty of amendment in others, for the sake of our own personal comfort. But have we reflected on this thing? What? — the faults which a man does not overcome in the interest of his own conscience, and his eternal safety, for the sake of his own soul, which, even on this earth, demands their conquest in the name of peace; for God's, who unceasingly exhorts him thereto, — shall he correct these because they inconvenience you? Do we not see him constantly wielding them against himself with an indisputable capability of self-injury?

It has often been said that self-interest governs the world. This is only true with many reservations. The free but perverted will, when cool, would gladly resolve to listen only to the voice of self-interest; but in evil, as in good, we must submit to our master. The freaks and vagaries of the passions soon defeat our purposes. If we look closely, we shall see that it is not so much interest as passion that governs men; and that passion almost always holds its ground.

Is there a scandal or an irregularity which has not its lesson? What does perfidy teach us? That God alone cannot lie! And ingratitude? That God only assumes the debts of those who have themselves forgotten them.

And for those griefs above all griefs, which have belied and destroyed every hope of happiness, and, gnawing into the heart, would have blighted and perhaps ruined it had not the divine sap lent its own life to the renewal of the nobler instincts, — why should any degree of wonderment mingle with a sorrow that is only too comprehensible? Do we not know that the human being is to find his centre, his true refuge, nowhere on this earth; and that, crossing like a dove the sphere of the affections, and finding his true end in none, he must needs mount ever higher before he can find rest? *Volabo et requiescam.*

"We seek to live in what we love."[1]

But when we perceive that, of so many lovers, there are so few whom their love has rendered happy, is it difficult to understand the scope of that law which brands, as sinfully and unlawfully employed, all strength which is wasted in glowing desires, in fixed and absolute preconceptions, and in what has been so well defined as "the envious poverty of an exclusive love"?[2]

---

[1] St. Augustine.   [2] M. Sainte-Beuve.

The sufferings of genuine sensibility, purified from the leaven of egotism, are of another sort; but the dangers of deception, — the heavy blows, the sad and sudden revelations, the wounds inflicted on a trust that can never be restored, — these, it is by no means spared. Reason may have controlled these sentiments; imagination may have but the slightest share in them; 'tis enough to have opened one's heart, to have rested on that of another, to have expected, to have hoped; and we lay ourselves open to those voluntary or involuntary wrongs, which reveal the weakness much more than the malignity of our nature. If it be true that all suffering originates in love of some kind, it is equally true that no love is free from suffering; and hence, if we abandon ourselves to it, do we not pave the way for our own mistakes, and make ourselves accomplices in our own deception, when what is infinite within us demands of one weak heart all the affection needed by our own?

Man would fain change the conditions of this mutable and perishable world, which is wrought out of vanity. This instinct of happiness, left to man with so wise and lofty a purpose, as a souvenir of the state whence he has fallen, and to which he aspires, — this very instinct, misunderstood as it is, tends incessantly toward making a heaven of earth, and a possession of what God merely lends us. The natural man is not exactly impious, but he is essentially idolatrous. His worship is always ready for the object of his taste or predilection. Instead of earning the happiness of heaven by effort, as a favor and compensation, he would gladly obtain it in this world by the haughty and imperious methods of an indomitable will. He deifies all that he loves, and will be all in all to what loves him; and if the end of it all be not some deadliest mistake, deception or imbitterment, yet the griefs which enervate and slowly consume, do not fail him.

This same instinct shows itself in those Utopian schemes, brilliant and impracticable, which deny at the outset, that sin is the point of departure for the human race, or its destination heaven. And so, building upon error, they arrive at absurd conclusions; as if the lot of man could be essentially changed while his heart remains the same!

Man is urged on by an insatiable desire for happiness. The social Utopia turned the world upside down, decreeing with criminal indifference the ruin, and even death, of the present generation, in view of a golden age, which it could only see in imagination across destruction and *débris*. Alas! even in the fruitful fields of high Christian hope, Faith, elsewhere submissive, allows the thread whereby the Church guides all her children through every labyrinth, to hang too loosely in the hands; and dreams at times of a new garment for this earth, preferring the transformation of the gloomy, shadowy dungeon to the joy of quitting it. Always this earth! Both with the millenarian who would make it the theatre of heavenly glories, and with the chimerical reformer who pursues the senseless dream of impossible equality and well-being. But this earth, which they would fain make a permanent abode, and the ultimate end of man's destiny, is but a temporary place of trial. It allows of no joy, save that of practical virtue; and of that foretaste of happiness that is given us that we may realize its insufficiency.

While we move in the world of impressions, and engage in the *mêlée* with all the blindness of improvidence, all appearances seem real: we close with the first comer, and self-possession deserts us in the storm of blows. But as the tumult subsides, the rapt thought regains its freedom. We observe, and by and by ask ourselves the reason why feelings are often so surely balked by facts; why so many joys are shipwrecked without storm or reef; why attempts of the most opposite nature are alike foiled by the results; what mean these perfectly natural causes, supernaturally employed; and, in short, the reason of the manifest impossibility of explaining any thing on human grounds. Thus are we put on the track of that Supreme Will, which acts at once conspicuously and mysteriously, stamping all its lessons with a twofold character, just as, in the words of Scripture, there is always an historical sense, and a mystical sense, which is its soul.

If, to these first revelations, succeed formidable and repeated trials; if these seemingly universal pains have a thousand keen and jagged points, whose existence we never suspect till their ordinary proportions receive a gigantic development, by this or that secret coincidence with the dispositions which render them special, incisive, and poignant; if these marvellous sorrows seem to have eyes which enable them to aim at the most vulnerable point, ears to detect each moan, lips wherewith to render their language more intelligible; if they find out sensitive spots in your nature, which you yourself had never perceived; if their action, in short, is at once all-torturing and all-illuminating; and if, approaching you in ever narrower and narrower circles, they leave you at last only space for sacrifice and self-abnegation, and air enough to breathe at God's side, are you not constrained to identify their author? Human nature is doubtless very sagacious, its arm is mighty to wound, but it strikes heavily in lieu of striking home; and how different is the intelligence which directs its blows from the firm, sure hand of the great Archer! . . .

At the culminating point of trial this consoling clairvoyance begins; for it is here that God reveals himself, beneath the mask of human dispositions which he moves, works, and directs to his own purposes. Here it is that all rebellion and impatience against the external agent seem to border on sacrilege; and the divine intervention becomes so manifest that, even in the form of chastisement, it strengthens our confidence, as once the monarch's presence sufficed to insure the pardon of the condemned.

While occupied with those who suffer, we come too close to those who cause suffering, not to address a few words to these also. If God knows how to extract good from evil; if relative good, with its richest consequences, may result from the sorrows we endure, — there is naught among all the marvellous transmutations, possible and providentially foreseen, which can reassure those who inflict suffering. They assume and keep the responsibility of their acts. The victim has often owed to the executioner the lofty rank he occupies, but the *rôle* of the executioner does not, therefore, become more enviable.

Here, then, is the miracle of resignation. It makes the sorrows we owe to personal agency transparent, and shows us God behind them. From the moment when we catch a glimpse of the Saviour through the light veil of men and events, the most intentional and direct offences and injuries are but the divine finger, indicating the way which leads to future bliss. Our griefs still cause us to suffer, but they have lost their sting. From the rank of masters our enemies have descended to that of instruments, and we see those obeying who dream that they command.

Yet, let us pause at that word *enemies*, nor allow it to have, in the pious heart, its too easy and common acceptation. An enemy? Of all accidents, this is the rarest. A restless and susceptible personality renders us hard and suspicious toward all with whom we come in contact. What is not humane appears hostile: we see a grim opposition in all unflattering impressions; and one needs but to overstep the bounds of equity to exhibit in our eyes a revolting severity. "Oh, my friends," cried Plato, "there are no friends!" "Oh, you who suppose yourselves my enemies," I would rather say, "you are not my enemies." You wound me and you rend me, and, it may be, you will kill me; but you see not, you know not, the evil that you do. Human levity, far more than human malignity, is the cause of all those sinister effects which we think to explain by hatred only. What enemy has ever done us more harm than we have done ourselves? and it is not exactly self-love that we lack.

The idleness and weakness which allow us to judge by deceitful appearances; the prejudice against which we will take no precautions; a failure in kindness and justice, such as the best and fairest-minded are not secure against, — what incentives to wrong, what snares to the feet of justice they are! And, among those who exercise influence or authority over others, there is but one step from a false judgment to the most appalling consequences.

We explain all things by malevolence; but to measure this malevolence by the magnitude of the evil we endure, is another of the illusions caused by our preoccupation with self. We always arm with wrath or hate the hand that strikes us; and, if the truth were unveiled, how would it surprise us to find that the arrows which pierce us were shot at random, and that not merely no remorse, but almost no thought, has been given to the moment which has caused us to undergo a thousand torments! Ah, how much light is spared to evil-doers, that they may not be as culpable as they are senseless!

Where is the man who is so unhappy as to know all the harm he has done? That the powerful should be thus ignorant, is but natural; but the least, the obscurest, have they this knowledge? Do I, O my God! — pitiful and utterly insignificant I, — do I know all the ills I have caused, the burdens I have made heavy, the hopes I have deceived, the abundance and bitterness of the tears I have caused to flow? Of all the mysteries of this life, the deepest is the entanglement of destinies. The possible range, the immediate effect, the remote consequences and the reaction of our faults, our example, our course of life; the countless times, and the thousand and one ways, in which we have injured interests, minds, souls, and — who knows? — perhaps even hearts that loved us, and were more deserving than we, — of all these things we are profoundly ignorant.

AIX-LA-CHAPELLE, Aug. 22, 1842.

CHAPTER VI.

HOW, IN THE WORLD AND OUT OF IT, EVERY THING AND EVERY BEING, EXCEPT MAN, ACCOMPLISHES GOD'S WILL, AND KEEPS IN THE PLACE ASSIGNED IT.

To walk in God's ways, to belong to him, to be what he has willed we should be, and one day to lose ourselves in him, — these are our only reasonable desires. All others, though natural, are only legitimate and permitted. If we cast an eye over the visible and invisible universe, — on the spiritual beings who occupy the space above us which separates earth from heaven, and on the animate creatures which move on its surface or in its bosom, — we behold an innumerable throng of creatures, differing among themselves in rank, right, and privilege, but all faithfully realizing the thought they represent, and content with the place assigned them.

Enclosed within their appointed spheres, they run their course; and the inherent power of each is displayed in due order and measure, by the regularity of its movements in relation to those harmonies which constitute the beauty and majesty of nature. Thus, the countless tribes of the celestial hierarchy — the happy immortals who have each their banner and their name — never dispute among themselves for glory and precedence. The direct tie which binds them to their Master suffices for their felicity; and they seek not to measuré it by any jealous comparison. Each sacred phalanx chants the Creator's praises with as much ardor as if it alone were called to celebrate them; and the angel choirs who glorify the everlasting beatitudes, and reveal the transports thereof, add to the number of their joys the adoration which they would fain infuse into all the universe.

Love in heaven seeks diffusion as much as the tender passion on earth desires to be exclusive. The children of light are true to its essence, which is lavished without loss, and enriched by accumulation. The souls of men, after they pass into celestial beatitude, abjure all rivalry, all ambitious instincts. Let us listen to the secrets of those happy souls, as revealed by their inspired song.[1]

---

[1] Dante, Paradiso, Canto III.

"Ma dimmi; noi che siete qui felici
Desiderate voi più alto loco
Per più vedere, o per più forvi amice.

Con quell' altr' ombre pria sorrise un poco
Da indi mi ripose tantò lieta
Ch' arder parea a' amor nel primo foco;

. . . . . .

Fratre, la nostra volonta quieta
Virtù di carita che fa volerne
Sol quel ch' anemo et a' altro non à asseta.

Se disiassimo esser più superne
Foran discordi gli nostri desideri
Dal voler di colui che qui ne cerne

Che vedrai non capere in questi giri."
. . . . . .

"Yet inform me, ye who here
Are happy, long ye for a higher place,
More to behold and more in love to dwell?

She, with those other spirits, gently smiled;
Then answered with such gladness, that she seemed
With love's first flame to glow: Brother, our will
Is in composure settled by the power
Of charity, who makes us will alone
That we possess, and naught beyond desire.
If we should wish to be exalted more,
Then must our wishes jar with the high will
Of Him who sets us here, which, in these orbs,
Thou wilt confess not possible."

Cary's Translation.

As we descend from higher to lower things, nature reiterates the same profound and positive teachings at each step of the scale. Every kingdom and every species, and every individual of such kingdom or species, remains within its own limits, without alteration or encroachment; and the different orders of nature touch, but do not mingle. Nowhere in nature do we find a tendency to quit the conditions on which existence has been received, in search of others, or to depopulate the lower ranks by an upward movement. Star, ocean, flower, and bird, all desire to be what they are, and proclaim their universal acquiescence in solemn and affecting language.

In truth, it is only by a fiction that we attribute will to the elements of which our universe is composed; but the order and regularity which they maintain, betray the ruling plan. And does not this plan give us the idea of God? The world and all that it contains being the expression of one thought and stamped with one seal, does it not say, — as each planet moves in its orbit, as the ocean obeys its bounds, as flower and bird everywhere reproduce the same spectacle of submission, — that God pursues the same course in the moral as in the physical world, and defines for nations, as for individuals, the limits, the duties, and the services that he imposes on them?

A submissive universe is assuredly a noble spectacle: but the universe has no will, — or, rather, its will, if it had one, would be chained; and God waits to be glorified by a free consent. And shall man alone interrupt, by his revolt and his impatience, a concert so sublime? . . .

When God speaks to us, and we choose rather to listen to the father of lies; when, instead of the beatitudes of the gospel, we value and pursue only those forms of prosperity which it disdains and teaches us to dread; when, instead of desiring that God's will may be done, we strive passionately to secure our own, — our instincts may be genuine, but they are perverted.

Man is not wrong to aim at happiness, but he errs in the means he employs to attain it. And nations fall into the selfsame snare, when they take ambition for their motive, and glory for their end, and trust in force, or in Utopian dreams.

And so, sometimes, we see revolt provoked, by intentions that are generous and upright, — only too human, — when nothing is ripe for the combat, nor for the consequences of victory, if it be won. The result is, that men do not know what to do with their own success, and turn against those who have secured it; or, on the supposition of a defeat, fatigue, humiliation, that brute force, which is confessedly weak, and the absence of that principle of duty, which alone can sustain, plunge them, first into discouragement, then, and soon, into dependence and slavery.

Doubtless some people are more to be pitied than others. There are those whose condition wounds the most indefeasible rights of conscience and reason, whose misfortunes are *immoral*, in that they entail consequences most deadly to the character; but time alone can lawfully right such wrongs. No true estimate has yet been made of what is needful to insure some sort of redress for the greatest excesses. Equity, as regards flagrant injustice, makes its way blindly in the mind of the masses, like a slow and gradual gestation; but its day will come.

Do not, therefore, construct an earthly Jerusalem, whence all ills are to be banished, and where all bliss as well as all goodness is to remain fixed for ever. It is an impious mistake to stifle the thought of heaven by striving to bring heaven down to earth. If we would lighten our exile, let us render our prison endurable: embellish it if we can, make it wholesome at all events, but let us not dream of transforming it into a palace and a tabernacle of cloudless happiness. No: that happiness awaits for its development new heavens and a new earth.

The attempt to realize any Utopia has almost always been a work of destruction. All ardent desires for happiness, pursued in defiance of duty or prudence, invariably become sources of calamity. All alike imply misapplied power, ignorance of size and proportion, and a blind encroachment of our present on our future lot. God has made the soul of man so large and deep, that it feels cramped, if we give it no opening to the infinite; and, be the case that of a nation or an individual, an explosion will ensue, after the deplorable fashion of all long-repressed power.

It cannot be too often repeated that we here represent the problem of living in one world, with the instincts of another; and the question to be solved is, how the child of eternity shall find the way to his royal home. All else is secondary.

In our own age especially, that desire to rise, which has never deserted human nature, has received an alarming development, — the result of the multiplied chances of elevation, which all perturbed epochs present. The craving to do something other than they are doing, and to rise above the condition of their fathers, is so general among men, that, if the power of action equalled the audacity of desire, the whole social hierarchy would be subverted, and the lower ranks would be utterly vacated.

To these incentives of pride is joined a vague unrest, — a longing like the sick man's, not to be better, but to be different. All that we have not, and all to which we aspire, becomes, along with the regrets to which we yield, the object of actual worship. Our will in such a case is an exact counterpoise to the destiny which God has appointed us. . . . Thus man — starting from a point, firm and indisputable, because it is within him, and is reproduced without exception in all his kind — misses his way, and fails of his end, or strays from it, because he neglects the star which might have guided him safely. The horizon toward which he steers, is a moving one, and conspires with all things else to beguile him.

Truth is one; but when it falls under the conditions of our complex nature, it is translated into mixed instincts, which fail to render its inspirations, and are misled by lying mirages. In what trifles do we make the happiness for which we were created to consist! How we degrade it! And the ever-insatiate ambition of new rank and honor, and that other ambition, less coarse, but quite as unchristian, of influence, success, and consideration; that longing to act upon minds, when it is not to God that we would lead them, — have we not here the rough sketch of that zeal for God's house, which devoured the prophet?

We want to be free, rich, happy, beloved, learned. These are perfectly legitimate desires; but the greater part of the time we cheat ourselves of freedom, wealth, happiness, love, and knowledge. What we seek in vain on earth, we should infallibly find in God. He spares no pains, surely, to put us again and again in the right way. He speaks to us as clearly by the aching void at our hearts, by the profound *ennui* which pursues us, by the blunders which we make for ourselves, and the deceptions which we owe to others, as by the unspeakable attractiveness of his grace. Unwilling either to comprehend heaven clearly, or to desire it strongly, we travesty it, in obedience to all the lures of passion.

Ah! believe me, it is best to have confidence in what *is*. What *is* has the force of law. What *is* has, if not the sanction of God, at least his permission. And what would we substitute for it? Our own ideas, which have deceived us a thousand times, and of whose range and consequences we are alike ignorant. If by chance we are actually left to choose, we hesitate and inquire in vain, and cannot compass the most trivial arrangement; and ever afterward our desire is for clear and sure views, when there is a question of any of those myriad combinations, whereby the throng of beings who describe the same orbit, fulfil, unconsciously to themselves, the designs of Providence.

We arrive, however unexpectedly, at a rigorous demonstration of the fact, that the object of our repugnance is almost always the very thing which is most indispensably and indubitably necessary to us. In these bonds, which seem to constrain too much your faculties, your instincts and your talents, you may be sure of moving easily, if they are imposed by duty. That devouring unrest of yours shall be a lamp to your feet. That affliction it was which alone could have made you break with the world, and enticed you from its influence.

We are thoroughly acquainted only with the annoyances of the part which we ourselves bear, the situation where *we* are, and the evil which oppresses *us;* but do not wisdom and good sense consist in the reflection that every lot has its trials, every situation its annoyances, and that every organization bears in its own breast the destructive principle? When you think of the obstacles in your path, and the griefs which cause you to suffer, and tell their number, however great it may be, can you not offset against them the infinitude of contrary chances?

Can you say, that if this grief, this anxiety, whose gnawing fixity absorbs you, were removed, you would be left for ever, or even for any great length of time, in entire satisfaction and profound security? And if, on the other hand, your suffering is to be continued or renewed in one way or another, — since suffering is the inevitable law, of what consequence, after all, are the manner and way?

When you undertake to work out your own destiny, you confide to your own single strength the care of softening its severity. God puts consolation only where he has first put pain, and causes his mercies to abound nowhere, save in the furrow traced by penitence and laborious effort. You are at once too poor and too great: too poor in your views, for they do not reach the true horizon; too great to be able to be your own reward.

Let us eliminate from our lives all that is not marked with the seal of the divine will. "Every man," says St. Gregory, of Nyssa, "is the painter and the sculptor of his own life." In the midst of the original endowments of destiny, over which we have apparently no control, we do not realize — weak, fettered, and clogged as we are — how great our power still is.

Man resisting God, is Satan in his colossal deformity. Man obedient, aids God in his work. Nature, when she issued from the hands of the Creator, obeyed once for all. Man's true glory is to obey God each moment and for ever.

Doubtless, it belongs to man to grow and mount unceasingly. The desire of development, but of an internal, purely moral, regular, and peaceful development, which is but the law that summons him to perfect his being, is in the front rank of his attributes. Observe it is only the inner man who can grow unceasingly, and has an indefinite capability of advancement. With the carnal man the case is exactly reversed. The confines of life and of matter hamper him on all sides.

Between these two contrary attractions, there is but one ambition worthy of us; that, namely, which insures our progress in the spiritual life. And even here we must consult the will of God, learn what he wants of us, and to what place he assigns us. Wherever it may be, we must be content therein. How dare we choose among the mansions of the heavenly Father? To be a worm of the dust in obedience to God's designs is better in the eyes of wisdom, than to have the lofty nature of angels, and be abandoned to one's self.

Humility is as becoming in sacred things as in all others. Let us check the vehemence of our desires, even when they take the form of a legitimate wish for greater perfection. Let us joyfully acquiesce in seeing the spirituality of our brethren surpass our own; and, without dwelling upon ourselves, let us be sensitive only about what honors God. He knows what we need, and to what he calls us; and he alone knows it. Thus, like any other master, he chooses his servant, and intends to be heard and served as pleases him, not as pleases the servant.

There is no method which the Scripture does not try to turn us from proud thoughts, even of good things; proud, not because they soar so high, but relatively to our own strength, which we ought to have been able to estimate more truly.

We are reminded of our powerlessness by every invitation which is given us to advance; and humility is always set before us as the palladium of our best intentions. A thousand passages of Holy Writ attest it.

One of the titles to the celestial pity adduced by the Royal Prophet is this: —

"Lord, my heart is not haughty nor my eyes lofty: neither do I exercise myself in great matters, nor in things too high for me."

"Surely I have behaved and quieted myself, as a child that is weaned of its mother: my soul is even as a weaned child."

And it is because he feels that God bears witness to that humility which he makes his sole claim, that he cries, in a transport of joy, —

"Let Israel hope in the Lord henceforth and for ever."

And does not the gospel in its turn admonish us that not one of us can add a cubit to his stature?

Happy dependence of our earthly condition, which, through the very need we have of blessing, renders the Benefactor more present and more dear! Blessed temporary indigence which enables us to say with St. Ignatius, "We lack much that we may not lack God."

Let the part which has been assigned us in this world be held very precious, even in its most insignificant details. Let us prefer, though we may not have chosen it, all that we must accept. Let the intellect be more and more reconciled to the lot of those little ones who have received such merciful promises; and let us shrink from envying the lot of the great to which such formidable menaces are attached. All may rise. All may fall. And what signifies being first or last in the eyes, or on the breast, of Him who is himself the beginning and end of all things.

O my God, I desire not the glory of heaven! I ask not to reign there, but only there to serve thee. Ah, if there were but lay-sisters in heaven, and I might be one!

CHAPTER VII.

THAT THERE IS AN EXCESS OF GRIEF WHICH BELIES THE WORDS OF SUBMISSION.

WE must not dissimulate the fact, that to abandon one's self utterly to excessive grief, and to consent to that excess, renders illusory all the words and deeds whereby we think to express resignation. What signifies submission on the lips, if resistance is alive in the depths of the heart,—if God is but a God who pronounces judgments, and our trust, reverential though it be, remains inert and sterile! Suffering is like death; it must be whether we will or no: but the distinguishing mark of the Christian is that he brings to necessity what transfigures and annihilates it.

Doubtless the Christian suffers. He suffers deeply; for there is dignity in suffering, and all dignities are his: nay, more, he suffers perpetually; for God, who made consolation, did not make oblivion. Yet while we acknowledge the suffering to which man is condemned by sin, the words of the holy books are explicit and unanimous in proclaiming the reign of joy in this vale of tears. "He that is of a merry heart," saith the preacher, "hath a continual feast." And does not the apostle command us to "rejoice evermore"? The saints speak the same language, "Let piety weep," said St. Paulinus, "but let faith rejoice evermore."

But would not the Scriptures, which reconcile all contradictions, here assert the most flagrant of all, were there not joys in piety which predominate over all afflictions, enveloping and clothing them anew, like that garment of immortality which, in the words of St. Paul, the mortal is to put on? Faith, in its various degrees, is also a tree which may be known by its fruits; so that we no longer sorrow "as those who have no hope," neither are disquieted like those who have no Father in heaven.

What changes are wrought in the mind by a single thought of Providence and immortality! What becomes of the present, when a single hope arises? God enters by means of his inspirations into the heart of the faithful, and graciously admits him to the closest familiarity with himself. And out of the heart of such a life, mingled in some sort with that of God, how can we fail to form judgments very different from those dictated by our abandoned and self-abandoning nature!

The sudden shock and sorrowful overthrow have, no doubt, great claims on the divine indulgence; yet, if piety is deep and mature, and that which constitutes spiritual age has naught to do with the number of the years, it should have insured the blessing and produced the effects peculiar to itself; gained in velocity so to speak, and even in spontaneity, and reduced, at least considerably, the number of our terrible surprises. It is well said that impressions do not reason; and what seals the true Christian with peculiar distinctness is not merely the way in which he resists grief, but the way in which it affects him.

The habit of pious moderation shapes the whole man anew, and insures the triumph of the power of Christianity; the latter being supernatural not only in the truth it teaches, but also in the effects to which it gives rise. If, in souls subdued and shaped to the sacred yoke of faith, the very first impulse may be loyal and submissive, has not God the right to demand as much when space for reflection has intervened, when some sort of order has succeeded to the perturbation, when, in a word, time, that mighty auxiliary of virtue, has been able to act?

What shall we say, then, of those deep ravages which men allow to be wrought within them? of those violent transports, those wasting and consuming regrets, those sorrows which are suitably borne externally, but carry on, all the same, a work of destruction at which the will either renders a kind of passive assistance, or calculates and applauds its effects with a sombre inner joy?

When excessive suffering causes death, even in the form of annihilation, to seem a deliverance, does not the fact reveal the guilty character of a grief which makes us abjure all our hopes? And is not that negative suicide, which is almost as grave a thing as the other, which is consequent upon sorrow long-continued, enervating, and wearing to the springs of life, — is it not a foe whom we should resist with all our might, if it plainly shortens or trenches on the days wherein God has doubtless planted a thousand germs of salvation?

Do we reflect how impious a death it may be to die of grief? Did any saint ever die so?

Men are peculiarly affected by this sort of death. They admire it with a pious idolatry, deeming it the apotheosis of human sensibility. But why not rather say with Saint Bridget, "The fools who cry, 'We would sooner die than yield our will!'" In vain do they say, with bowed heads, yet unwilling to lift up the prostrate soul, "We adore the ways of God, and he alone is master." Ah, however reverent their silence or their speech, conscience owns that this abandonment to sorrow, this uncontrolled anguish, has but one true name, and that is — murmur!

And this murmur is not merely a plaint; it is, though inarticulate, an accusation. For do we not accuse God of being an unjust Master, when we intimate that he lays on his servants burdens too heavy to be borne, — burdens which their virtue may indeed support, nor suffer the escape of a groan, but which crush them none the less? Do we not accuse God of ingratitude when we allow it to be supposed that he does that of which many, even corrupt men, are incapable, and that he suffers those to fail who have given themselves to him?

And when the enemies of that God of justice and also of meekness laugh at his thunderbolts, dispute his benefits, proclaim his supreme indifference, you, his believers, his servants, his friends, know not how to defend him. You leave the impression that, in truth, he can neither love his own, nor provide a secret counterpoise to their visible afflictions; that he deigns neither to strengthen nor to sustain; that, consequently, we can feel sure of nothing but his blows; that, powerless or faithless, he either cannot or will not comfort us; and, finally, that the considerations of which faith is born, — endowed, perchance, with a feeble and limited action, — cannot cope with cruel events and severe wounds. God will justify himself one day, but we must justify him here.

And that prostration which succeeds acute suffering, that melancholy depression, no longer characterized either by the startling signs or the dull mutterings of the storm, but which resolves itself into a condition in which the soul seems overspread with a mourning veil, is that more legitimate in the Christian's eyes? What! you attempt to set forth the shining truths of the divine word, the magnificence of its revelations, the mercy of its designs; and, at the same time, you allow the suspicion that God cannot console, that he has no treasure in reserve wherewith to soften his sternness, and that the sincerest piety is, after all, as ineffective as the vainest philosophy.

This permitted depression, submissive as it may appear, is none the less a guilty defection, and a silent protest against God's decrees. Ah! you who love him, and desire his glory and triumph, reflect that, when sadness overpowers you, you become the place, the occasion, the accomplices of his defeat; that it is the very God who is vanquished in your persons as often as your love and faith fail to rise above your grief! Ah! how can we help overcoming sorrow, when God is for us and against sorrow? Does not our weakness betray a languishing faith, and prove that, though there may be resignation in the conscience, it has not yet penetrated to the heart; that is to say, that the self-immolated victim has so much of life left, that rebellion still ferments within him?

Let, then, the soul that has been touched by grace make haste to overcome these failings; and, more faithful than Ananias, yield up that secret, smarting grief which the instinct of a passionate bitterness would fain make the heart's last idol.

When the wind of earthly lust still fans the face; when we turn our eyes on perishable things; when we sit down at the feast of the impious, and lend our ears to the accents of the doubter; when, in short, we seek "the happiness of men," — then it is that we know sorrow. But for him who loves and follows thee, O my God! grief, a phantom of man's raising, does not exist. There is naught for him but love, hope, joy, submission, and sacrifice. Grief is vanquished as well as death.

Or, rather, this grief changes its character, and recalls the sweet and sad solemnity which the Church throws around the funeral rites of little children. It is death; but the words and the chants express the assurance of a blessed life, from which a light veil only divides us. The chants are sad; the exile knows no other; but there is nothing woful or heart-rending in them. Sin is not there. We shed many tears, but there is no mourning; and, for prayers, there are canticles of joy.

Even so, it seems to me, we find in the innocent little one, lying motionless in his coffin, embalmed in flowers, a fitting emblem of the Christian's grief. For the child, there is the possession of God; for the Christian's sorrow, there is the certainty of one day possessing Him. The child has gone to God; God will come to the expectant sorrow. Sorrow knows that he will come; and, though he delay awhile, still it waits, for he will surely come. *Veniet et non tardabit.* And, like the Church, who gives her voice for these sinless souls, who form the milky way of the heaven of souls, Christian sorrow — patient of suffering, impatient of deserving to suffer — is more ready with ascription than with invocation.

The effects of faith are not strictly confined to the realization of its threatenings and promises concerning a future life. In this world, also, faith bears blessed fruit; and the earthly happiness of the true Christian, however inferior in dignity, enters quite as much into the plan of the divine Legislator. . . .

This religion of self-denial protects all that it regulates, confirms all that it approves, and fortifies all that it restrains or limits. The less we aim at happiness, the more it causes us to encounter in the world; and this happiness is increased in proportion as we strive to lift the heart rather than to satisfy it. Christianity treats happiness precisely as it treats the body. It forbids man to give more than a secondary place to either. Knowing their dubious fidelity, it wills that he should watch them both, always subjugate and sometimes sacrifice them; and, in a word, that, in his relations with them, he should continue to be lord and master.

Christianity, which seems to despise happiness, and

treat the body as an enemy, honors the one and defends the other, more than any other *cultus* or system was ever known to do.

What a divine character Christianity imparts to earthly happiness! What a fond sanction it gives to all the heart's lawful affections! How many incentives its words supply to constant and ever-growing love!

And this poor human body, which, one would think, Christianity cared only to subdue, what system, even of those who deified it, has ever awarded it such true honor as the Word, who associated it with his own divinity, who promises it resurrection, and who summons it by those sacraments, whereof the nature is always twofold, to a share in the most marvellous blessings which can descend upon the earth?

God neither hates nor despises aught that he has created. Nothing is too little or abject for him to raise and purify. In his severities, it is not vengeance which is expressed here below, nor even justice: it is always his love. It is ever by a less degree of suffering, that the sinner is indemnified for the deserved suffering which he undergoes.

The whole Catholic system has been so arranged as to come to the aid of the human creature, in the twofold aspect of his life here and his life beyond. Its ethics, its precepts, its counsels, have no other end than this.

Those virtues which have been exalted above the rest, and called the three divine virtues, because of their regenerative power, contain the principle of the greatest help and comfort that man can receive.

Faith! — to trust, — in a word, to lean, — to act under an ever-open eye, and an arm always ready to lift you up. To feel yourself summoned within by a voice whose accents never fail to move you in the tempest or the calm, in joy or in tears; to have a witness who attends you, a defender who shields you, a confidant who hears you; a friend never absent, never dull, never mute, who not merely listens but answers, who can never be either ignorant or abstracted, and who shows you in the world a fleeting vision, and reveals that eternity where joy awaits you.

From the sweet and smiling picture which even Error has drawn of *Hope;* from the undeniable benefits of her merely natural action; from the flowers with which she can strew the saddest life; from her prism so rich in hues; from that fidelity to her vocation which renders her the constant and unfailing companion of man from the cradle to the grave, — it is easy to imagine what Christian hope must be: holy hope with the terrestrial element gloriously transfigured. No illusions does she invoke. She requires only truth, — that truth which is ever fruitful and inexhaustible. Placed between Faith and Charity, Christian Hope is the reward of the one and the prelude to the other; or, rather, these three heavenly sisters mingle their rays, and borrow splendor from one another.

If God had but permitted man to love him, it would have been much. But, though he has everywhere deposited the germ of this *love*, he develops, trains, and feeds it with peculiar care in the hearts of the children of his Church. Who does not know that the child learns to love only at its mother's knee? There only are those chaste pleasures prepared which insure unfailing happiness and love.

And of these three forms of human felicity, — faith, hope, and charity, — Christianity makes duties, that none may fail thereof save by his own fault. And, in the practical life of piety, what pains are taken to warn us, to shield us from ourselves, to apprise us of our dangers, to defend us at the tribunal of pardon, to intoxicate our souls at the sacred table, to ravish the imagination, to please the senses, to speak to the intellect, and console the heart!

And, if the lyre within accords ever so imperfectly with the divine diapason, what a delicious calm there is in self-possession, in the feeling of a harmonious equilibrium between all the powers of our being! What freedom within us thenceforth, and how rich and beautiful the world appears to our serene and unembarrassed gaze!

When the heart is fervid and full of pious ecstasy, how enchanting are the aspects of nature, which reveal God so sweetly, in his wonderful works!

What resources in labor! What varied treasures offered by art, science, and, above all, by study, which responds so perfectly to our active curiosity, revealing, moreover, that heaven where the bliss of knowledge comes next to that of love!

And this for all, without exception or privilege, for peculiarly favored situations! This is our share in the universal patrimony; the common fund, the heritage of all, and especially of those who, though they share largely in so many blessings, are often most disposed to slight them!

The instinct which causes us to pursue happiness is a proof of the reality of happiness. It is hardly to be supposed that we imagine something which neither has been nor ever will be. It would be creation outside of nature. If the iron moves and is strongly attracted, it is because the magnet exists.

That problem of the supreme good, which absorbed the attention of antiquity, is wonderfully solved by Christianity, which reveals to us at once a perfectly beautiful life, and a perfectly desirable death. It would seem, at first sight, that if the aspect of life were fair, we should dread death, which is its term; and that, on the other hand, the desire of death must discourage and disenchant us in respect of life. From the stand-point of humanity, whose esteem centres in transitory good, it could not be otherwise: it would certainly be an attempt to reconcile incompatibilities.

But under the Christian system, glowing aspirations can have but one legitimate object, — eternal bliss. The happiness we hope in death, and that which we receive from life, without being identical, are not strangers to each other, for the possession of God is the foundation of them both.

Death desirable outside of Christianity? Only the unfortunate can admit the thought, and that under inconceivable conditions of trouble and despair! They look upon it as an end; but for the Christian it is at once the beginning and the fulfilment of all the hopes which cross the realm of time.

To render death perfectly desirable, it must needs be that, as with the many saintly souls whose passage from this world to the next has been one song of deliverance, our wealth should be laid up elsewhere than here below, and our hearts following our treasure. And, that life may be always and supremely beautiful, devotion and self-sacrifice must be of the number of our joys; the vastness of our aim must react, at every step, upon the distance to be traversed; and our personal efforts, the miracles of grace, illusions destroyed and true blessings truly appreciated, — must concur to form a reality of blessedness, whereof the world is profoundly ignorant, and which has been enjoyed only by that multitude, that no man can number, who people the celestial city.

"The angels," said St. Gregory the Great, "carry their paradise with them wherever they are sent by

God, because they never cease to be united to him." This is the secret of lasting joy.

Christianity is not a barren, speculative theory. Every one of its dogmas implies a virtue, which is commanded to manifest itself by results.

In the language of men, whatever is not flagrant rebellion is denominated resignation; but, in sober Christian speech, the words used to express ideas should, as in the sacramental formulas, effect what they signify. Here, then, what is required is not merely internal acquiescence, but that living acceptance which shall produce its proper effects of light and love.

Nothing can come, without your consent, between the *thought* of the mind and the *wish* of the heart.

In that spiritual realm, that domain which none but yourself can penetrate, you have only yourself to conquer: you are king because you are free. Nought can hinder you from conforming or degrading your sentiments, or raising them to the height of your guiding principles.

Your outward behavior is susceptible of a thousand interpretations which may serve as your excuse; but, in the depths of your being, you are entirely responsible for the impulses you obey. There, the slightest discord between what you say and what you feel constitutes a lie; the least weakness, a prevarication; the least demur to one of God's commands, a denial of his providence.

And if a wish long since formed, or an engagement undertaken, already bind you; if, moved by a sacred charm, you have employed those words, so tender and sweet to the lips, of entire conformity, of surrendered will, and irrevocable abandonment to the divine wishes; — What do I say, if you have ever declared to God that his will was yours, and that, having yielded once for all, your heaviest punishment would be to resume guidance of yourself; if these unreserved, unconditioned, unalterable words have been uttered, believe me, that to give, and yet withhold, will avail with God least of all.

With ability, it may be possible to prevent men from suspecting aught but what we show them; but a jealous God sees what we withhold from him most clearly in what we offer.

And where your submission is judged sufficient at all points, are you not inclined and impelled to do more than is required of you, to clear the distance which separates precept from counsel, the obligatory from the optional? The precept is only strict justice, as we conceive it from its accomplishment under the ancient law; but counsel with its free spaces is the new law, whereby we receive the adoption of sons.

All science has its definitive experiments, which give it the force of law.

In the science of Christianity, it is perhaps the Christian's happiness which furnishes the most incontestable evidence of the fidelity of God to his promises. Reflection shows us that there is a universal argument in favor of the truth, — accessible to all men at all times, but which belongs exclusively to the servants of that adorable truth; displaying all its beneficence and profoundly logical power, defying all contradiction; the irresistible homage rendered by the servant to his master; and that argument is the internal but visible bliss enjoyed by the true Christian.

Outside of Christianity, happiness cannot be absolute, for nowhere else is there a sufficient counterpoise for the immense weight of human misery. Here only, there is a lever powerful enough to lift our fallen nature to those immeasurable heights where the world's true proportions are revealed.

A free spirit, a sweet and even temper, a countenance of content, express order without and peace within. This steady and sustained bearing — which is not merely the effort of a few moments, but the reality of all, since it cannot come by nature, which is ever full of vicissitudes — must be attributed to grace; or at least to some superior principle, which the most prejudiced are forced to acknowledge.

Happiness is à thing so uncommon, and so highly esteemed, that it cannot be seen without causing remark, without raising the question whence it comes and whither it goes. The most uncultivated as well as the most refined minds, those whose nature is most serious as well as those least inclined to trouble their heads about abstract truth, are forced to seek for the source of so rare a prodigy.

Observe that, in consequence of social degeneracy, the other means which truth has at command have acquired an infirm, intermittent, questionable character. Speech? How it has been abused! Does it not often add to the difficulty of comprehension? Acts? It so happens that they excite equal distrust, so nicely can they be calculated to conceal personal interest. Beliefs? They too can be feigned in the interest of order and public peace. The imagination may be enthralled by the beauties of religion as well as by many others. Large and bold openings may be made into all the realms of the sublime, without carrying to the mind the conviction of a single, focal centre, burning and blessing at the same time.

In speculative statements, every thing may be controverted and rendered debatable; but when, to the eyes of this greedy or prosperity-laden world, which is, none the less, sad, unquiet, weary, accustomed to see in every rule an insupportable yoke, and in the life of duty only a fastidious monotony; when you, the representative of all that world rejects and despises, show that you at least possess the happiness which it seeks and from which it flies, imagine the impression you produce! What sight like that of the flower of peace, the bright serenity of the Christian under the pressure of calamity, privation, age, illness, and the sombre elements which go to make up the life of man!

A joy which is rooted within, which neither displays itself nor hides itself, but merely suffers observation, whose permanence has already something of celestial immutability, bewilders men, yet causes them to reflect. They find themselves at a loss how to explain, on human grounds, so strange a phenomenon. They begin to comprehend that it must have some mysterious and divine element; and the hidden agent of these marvellous effects comes near revealing his deity, as Jesus did to the centurion at the crucifixion.

Yes: there is, in this world, a silent apostolate, a living, legible creed, an incessant and persuasive preaching; and it is the natural irradiation of a deep and genuine content. Christians and children of the Church, the joy which we taste in her service is, of all our acts of homage, the least open to suspicion, the most just, the most grateful. Never will the immortal hopes to which we offer the sacrifice of our piety be so clearly announced by our speech, as by the contrast between our known sufferings, and the radiant tranquillity of that repose which passes from the heart into the face.

Whatever trials we may undergo, however we may be stripped of consolation, support, and desert, is there not left us the lot of those stars of which the Prophet speaks, "which, being bright, and sent to do their offices, are obedient."[1] Let us ever be ready to say with Bourdaloue, "I know not, O my God! whether Thou art content with me: I acknowledge freely that Thou hast reason to be otherwise; but as for me, O my God! I must confess to Thy glory, that I am content with Thee, and that perfectly. It matters little to Thee whether I am this or no; but, after all, it is the most glorious testimony that I can render, for to say that I am content with Thee is to say that Thou art my God, since none but a God could content me."

CHAPTER VIII.

IS RESIGNATION COMPATIBLE WITH PRAYER THAT GOD WILL REMOVE THE EVIL WHICH AFFLICTS OR THREATENS US?

SUCH a doubt could only occur to those who, with lofty intent, should essay to walk in the way of the perfect. It is akin to those generous illusions which have misled many souls, and caused them to miss their mark by overshooting it.

---

[1] Baruch.

Motionless and speechless, renunciation often becomes a snare, like disinterestedness, to ardent love. But Christianity is not a series of initiations, in which, keeping no account of progress made, we cast aside, like useless scaffolding, all the methods which we employed to arrive at the point last gained.

All the teachings of Christianity, like its dogmas and its duties, have, so to speak, the simultaneity of God himself. The greatest virtues will never excuse the lack of the least: martyrdom, gloriously met, would not exempt from obedience to the Church's lightest law; and, if you had climbed to the third heaven, its ecstatic orisons would not enable you to dispense with the prayer of the humble. Every day, morning and evening, you would still need to say, "Forgive me my debts as I forgive my debtors. Lead me not into temptation;" still beginning anew where all the world begins in your obedience to God's commands, though, by his goodness, you may have been called upon to speak, and to feel better than any other.

But, aside from the moral, intellectual, and philosophical considerations which run parallel with the route which faith alone can discover to our eyes, we must remember that, in Christianity, whose teachings are essentially historical, authoritative example constitutes law.

So when we see Jesus pleading with his Father to remove the cup from his lips, or crying out upon the cross with a groan of despair, "My God, why hast thou forsaken me," can the Christian doubt that his adorable Master has sanctioned prayer even as a plaint, an inarticulate wish, or a cry for help by human sensibility?

We see the Church praying for the deliverance of Peter, as erewhile she prayed in the upper chamber for purely spiritual blessings; and it seems as if prayer were an act so excellent that God blesses it even when he will not hear.

It is not, of course, to rebellion that God says, "Ask, and ye shall receive," but to submission "Knock!" He says, moreover, And if the door at which you knock resists, your words, your entreaties will none the less be reckoned in the supply of other needs, which you, perchance, do not see so clearly. Prayer fructified by grace is the mediator between man and Christ, as Christ himself is the mediator between God and the world.

God has appointed honors and rewards for the exercise of the virtues. He has invested these with prerogatives, but prayer he has treated more munificently. Visibly modifying under its influence the severity of his decrees, allowing himself to be swayed by intercession, he gives it, we may venture to say, a claim upon himself. Thus, not only does prayer move and shake God in his designs, and induce him to suspend their execution, but human prayer is also at the bottom of almost every miracle. It would seem as if God, after creating the obedience of the saints, longed to taste its delights.

For how has he shown himself to us? "Obedient unto the death of the cross." And since then? At the voice of the priest, he descends to the altar. At the voice of man, he heals and makes amends.

"When I see," said St. Catherine of Genoa, "how lovingly and carefully he makes all possible provision for leading us to his own country, I am, as it were, constrained to say, that this good God seems to be our servant."

In cases of extraordinary favor and marked predilection, we can hardly suppose that God, in whom there is always a union of knowledge and foreknowledge, is not influenced by the merit of him who is their object, and that the latter does not prevail, up to a certain point, by prayer.

Miracles are earthly in their nature. We have no reason to suppose that there are any in heaven. Miracle enters into the number of our prerogatives, our chances, and, consequently, of our hopes. Let us try to deserve to have this divine force pause at us, — that God should permit us to be its conductors; and as, under the ancient law, all who belonged to the numerous and royal house of David, might hope to give birth to the Messiah, let us strive to render less impure the channels through which the divine pity may flow, either to stop with us or to pass on.

Moreover, how can prayer ever be qualified as inopportune? Is it not always the highest glorification of God's power?

It would be a false spirituality, indeed, which should lead us to consider, in the light of an imperfection, a recourse to prayer in the case of those preferences which pertain to the world of sense. Human things, aside from those which must be rejected as bad or suspicious in themselves, are divided into superior and inferior, — into interests which affect the heart, and such as appeal only to the vanity.

Earthly prosperity excites this vanity; not so the profound and legitimate sentiments of the heart. Why, then, should we not intercede for the objects of our pure and lively affection, with regard not merely to their spiritual, but to their human interests; not merely that we may win for them immortal life, but that we may protect and prolong their days upon the earth.

And, as we pray for others, why should it not be lawful to pray for ourselves? — to ask of God to avert the misfortune which we dread, and continue us the comfort to which we cling?

The God of the Christian is not the passionless, pantheistic God of nature; nor must the Christian incur the risk of mistaking insensibility for virtue. He is greater than the world, but he shrinks not from contact with it; and, following the example of his Master, he loves it, that he may bless, and, if possible, save it. In the midst of his most glowing ardors, the Christian acknowledges that the interests which touch us most nearly are the most salient and clearest to our eyes; he perceives, moreover, the worth which resides in inferior blessings, when we possess them lawfully, and enjoy them discreetly, and does not invent a gratuitous incompatibility between our salvation, and what God gives us for our happiness.

So true is this, that often we may safely say that the loftiest purposes have been effectually subserved by temporal goods. Thus, the life of one is a powerful aid; the health vouchsafed another has been the means of many a worthy deed; and the fortune well employed has covered more than one transgression.

Prayer, which is both spiritual and emotional, is the manifestation of the two men, whom the best of us bear within. The one represents too often the unweakened opposition of nature; the other springs to the eternal spaces. The one still clings to his possessions, and reviews his past as a part of himself; the other, self-emancipated, betakes himself to hope, rather than memory. The one is accessible on all sides, and impressible at all points; the other, self-collected, — living a life of profound and inexhaustible spiritual intensity, and integrity.

These two men are not always at ease with one another; nor are we at ease with them. Yet, however great the apparent difference in their centres of gravity, they both pray, and God hears them. The prayer of the first is always articulate: that of the second is voiceless and speechless; and, while the former grows weary of what it calls its useless desires, the latter never wearies, for its desire is eternity, — eternity, whose inspirations bring with them the patience of the saints! If we do not already belong too clearly and decidedly to one or the other of these two men, let us attempt to conciliate and make them live in harmony. Let the one elevate and purify the other, while the latter insures, by slightly retarding, his brother's progress.

God desires us to speak to him without reserve. Those goods which are capable of becoming objects of sacrifice, need none the less have been, originally, objects of perfectly lawful desire. If we have smothered longings, let them not be such as we have concealed, but such as we have renounced. We ought to be able to bring all that is within us to God, and surrender it to his influence, either for opposition or consecration.

He not only permits, but commands, us to reveal

to him our needs, our desires, our aversions, our sorrows. He even goes so far as to allow us to tell him our most fugitive and idle thoughts. Yea, even dreams and chimeras we may unfold, nor fear the accusation of audacity.

If it is true that "God punishes unwise prayers by hearing them," as the Scripture says, it is not the prayer itself, nor its imperfection, nor even our error, which can produce such an effect; for God in his goodness often allows us to be innocently mistaken; and if the fulfilment of our wishes comes in the form of punishment, it comes as the consequence of faults and errors far other than those of imperfect, familiar, and inconsiderate prayer.

If we reveal our hearts to him, we make sure of the strongest claim on his indulgence. We may do this unreservedly. God lays no snares for our feet. It is a beautiful and affecting miracle of the divine economy, that, spite of the immeasurable distance that divides us, God can act on us, and we on him.

The sweetest charm of human relations is doubtless the twofold influence mutually exercised by those who love; the solicitude and affection constantly expressed by a movement of action and reaction. And when we reflect that the spiritual life is nothing else than this; that it is all comprised in the grace which descends, and the love which ascends with corresponding fidelity; that God has so arranged the affairs of this world, that his intercourse with his creatures may have all the tenderness and intimacy of two hearts that meet and mingle, — we know not in what words to depict our gratitude.

God first loved us. He came to dwell with us. He is still in our midst. It is his delight to converse with man. "*Deliciæ meæ esse cum filiis hominum.*" He takes pleasure in intercourse with his children, whom he is ever returning to seek. Not only does he say *Ephpheta*, not merely does he open their ears: he loosens the tongue, and applies his redemptive virtue to every infirmity. What, then, is there to hinder so sacred a familiarity?

God would be swayed, God would be sued: it is due to his justice, and his original designs for man. God wills that Moses, and the man who was born blind, Nineveh, and the woman of Canaan, the town, the world, all ages, and all tongues, should pray. The Scriptures reproduce this truth under every variety of aspect, because prayer may assume any form and any voice, and be translated into any and all the acts which emanate from the heart of man. Thus almsgiving is prayer; penitence is prayer; sacrifice, endurance, submission, — all alike pray. Every conscientious meditation on our faults, every effort at amendment, every conquest over self, is prayer, and avails as such.

We aspire through prayer; we respire through resignation. Let us pray with all the intensity of which we are capable, with no fear that our trust will be belied. God regulates, directs, and purifies our ardor, but never checks, in order to perfect it. Only let us be watchful of our most urgent entreaties and eager desires, lest they interfere with our submission.

Prayer, with the Christian, is the calm and confident gaze of the child upon his father; of the sick man who discloses his malady, and interrogates his physician; of the friend who invokes his friend's presence: because all help is therein implied. When our desires are of a mixed nature, we must see to it that the void of our longings is not filled with the *débris* of partially consumed passions; and that a blind and persistent wish for success does not induce, in the course of its conflict with obstacles, those violent internal oscillations, which seem to threaten us at once with conflagration, and with darkness.

Let us pray; but let us pray according to the will of God, and in his spirit. To reveal our wishes, to hope, and to trust, is holy, pious, filial; but to reckon on the fulfilment of those wishes, and expect it as if that fulfilment were our due, is quite another thing. It is to pass from the love which believeth all things, and hopeth all things, to an irreverent and exacting mood, in which we show no proper sense of divine things. To expect is to demand God's coming; it is to give him our time, instead of accepting his. Adorable, even in his merciful tardiness, his goodness defers what it seems to refuse.

CONCLUSION.

. . . Suffering is profitable unto all things. Suffering teaches us how to suffer, to live, and to die. . . . Even if we could enter heaven by any other door than that of tribulation, our very love for God should deprive us of all thought or desire of so doing; for it is thus that our divine Master, and, after him, all the saints, have entered, bearing the cross, and treading a way strewn with thorns.

What examples are they, which the Scripture proposes for our imitation? Are they not those of hearts ready for every species of heroic sacrifice and self-immolation? Could suffering impose a check on Abraham or on Job? Did not grief wring from David his most magnificent utterances; and have not all the martyrs of the new law had one and the same experience of trial?

Is it not suffering, which, more than all other agents, tends to identify the feelings of the Saviour, and those of his ransomed creature, — which enables us to realize the miracle of assimilation? In what other aspect could our lives resemble that of Christ?

How else could our souls be identified with his, and attain to a comprehension of it? What have we of the sanctity, the profound condescension, the burning love of Jesus? And what has he of our pride, our laxity, our ingratitude, our rebellion?

Apart from grace, nothing, save suffering and its mighty plenitude, can fill the abyss between the God-man and his imitators. It is through suffering that God is most human. It is through suffering that man comes nearest to God.

Ask of the earthly affections, whether the dread of suffering ever hindered a generous soul in its love, and whether an infallible sign of the heart's interest be not the utter contempt of obstacles and sacrifices.

And then it would be vain to deny that there is in our nature a certain inclination towards suffering, — a kind of stray echo, as it were, of that primordial justice, which devotes us to expiation.

And so, despite our greed of happiness, despite our repugnance toward trials that are only too needful, all our joys end in satiety; and there is not a lofty, deep, or pure sentiment of our nature, which pleasure does not affect with a sacred sadness.

This secret charm of ineffable unrest mingles with the affections of all rare spirits. The elements of gladness and of melancholy exist in the same heart, and often side by side. They mingle with its substance; and, if mutually contradictory, so much the better do they symbolize the blessed inconsequence of our twofold nature.

In the midst of all the pursuits of pleasure and ambition; in the midst of every variety of vain and false estimate, — it is those who run the career of the prosperous, who are surest to be devoured by disgust of the same, under the very eyes of the giddy and envious public.

But question the pious souls, and they will tell you of the wealth, the life, the peace borne on the breast of that river of God, whose stream is always full. Oh why is not love more beloved? Desolation and sterility would vanish from the earth! . . .

Doubtless there would be found an astonishing number of minds ready to proclaim the beauty of the divine law, and the magnificent authority of its purposes, if the splendors which enchant the poet, and the speculative truths which fascinate the philosopher, were not accompanied by a severe code of morals, and the duty of self-renunciation and humility. When man is in the truth, the leadings of the heart's inclinations coincide with those of reason, as consulted by an unbiassed mind.

Ah, how happy and how great would humanity be, if able to translate into persevering action its vague instincts, its fleeting emotions, its passing aspirations towards the heavenly country! What a sight would not this earth present, if all who waste themselves in fruitless labor were striving to comprehend God! — to impart the joy he gives, to gather in from all quarters his children, his worshippers, and his elect; and to reveal to so many unconscious hearts that they have what they seek!

How full of rapture would be this noble destiny, — this so natural and powerful manifestation of the inner life! It would be the soul's hosanna sung in every metre; it would be a living and sublime lyric, a new hymn, a universal language, in which the succession of our deeds would unceasingly express the glory of God.

"Do you not feel," said Saint Madeleine, of Pazzi, "the infinite sweetness that is contained in those dear words, 'the divine will'?"

How easy it is to understand that holy bishop who, forgetting, or abdicating his own individuality, desired men to call him by no other name than this, *Quod Deus vult.* . . . Is there in all the world a tenderer prayer, or one more impressed with divine sympathy, than this, — "My Father, thy will be done"? A prayer which God himself has taught us, a talisman which enables us to banish his justice and summon his love. "Thy will be done"! Incessant miracle of a God who deigns to will, and a rebellious creature rising to the height of obedience! A sovereign prayer in its seeming self-annihilation.

O will of Him we love, which is always known, though not always understood; will, whose justice we may confide in, whose mysteries we adore; will which, to gain heaven, we would not intercept; adorable will, law of all beings, beatitude of the elect; will which constitutes the glory of the place which it assigns, and the power of the sacrifices it commands, — will of my God, involve mine own, more swiftly than the world issued from chaos, or the light sprang forth at thy voice, or than the joys of heaven cause the saints to forget the gloom of the passage thither. Will of my God, be mine, and continue till my latest breath to initiate me into the secret of thy growing delights!

Cambridge: Press of John Wilson and Son.

www.ingramcontent.com/pod-product-compliance
Lightning Source LLC
Chambersburg PA
CBHW031350230426
43670CB00006B/486